GEOGRAPHIC
SOUTH POLE
9'301 ft, 2,835 m

POLAR PLATEAU

TEAM SCOTT
76 DAYS 920 M
UNSUPPORTED
ARRIVING ON THE
17th JANUARY 2012
EXACTLY 100 YEARS
AFTER SCOTT

...GEN

...ARCTIC

CLOUDMAKER
MOUNTAIN

MT DARWIN

MOUNTAINS

SHACKLETON
INLET

BARNE INLET

920
MILES

MT
DISCOVERY

MINNA
BLUFF

TAYLOR VALLEY

...ORE ...ER

...ELF

SCOTT'S DISCOVERY HUT

HUT
POINT

SCOTT'S HUT
CAPE EVANS

MT EREBUS

SHACKLETON'S HUT

ROSS
ISLAND

TEAM SCOTT

...ARRIER

SEA

Plan D

Plan D
Building Your Resilience in the Face of Adversity

Paul 'Vic' Vicary

Dedication

To those people who have influenced, inspired and supported me in writing this book:

My dear late father, Eric Vicary;
my mother, Beryl Vicary,
who helped me become the person I am today;
the late Henry Worsley, a true polar explorer,
inspiration and legend;
good friends, Martin Rae and Mark Wood;
My constant rock of support, my wife Hanna (and the children).

Forewords

As a patron for this North Pole expedition, it is my pleasure to see this book in print. Plan D *depicts a modern-day polar story which, although it didn't go according to plan, is worth telling to understand why this happened. The team's mission was to report back what they witnessed during the expedition as they persevered to get onto the Arctic Ocean and to reach the Geographic North Pole. This book is part of that report, describing and illustrating what they witnessed and, most importantly, what is happening around the polar region.*

However, the book is much more than a simple report. It tells of the need for resilience in the face of adversities and coping in a crisis... highly relevant as we all travel through the current COVID crisis. It might even help you achieve your own 'North Pole'! Sadly, the climate crisis is much bigger than all of this, and to this end Plan D *raises awareness of the desperate plight of our planet.*

Sir Ranulph Fiennes, British explorer described as
"the world's greatest living explorer"

The sheer difficulty these days of reaching even the start point for a North Geographic Pole expedition says much about the world's fast-changing environment – the Arctic Ocean and its floating ice-reef ecosystem. Vic Vicary's ambition for a coast-to-Pole expedition to provide an eye-witness account deserves praise. That he achieved as much as he did is a tribute to his trademark determination.

Pen Hadow, Arctic explorer, the only person to have trekked solo
and unsupported from Canada to the Geographic North Pole

A fascinating read. Vic describes the extreme challenges of navigating the Arctic and bears witness to the striking realities of climate change – this is a story that needs to be shared.

Levison Wood, a British Army officer and explorer best known for his
extended walking expeditions in Africa, Asia and Central America

Contents

We were flown back to Barneo Ice Station, but as we looked down we saw the horrendous impact of the climate crisis. It was awful, with large cracks, broken ice, and simply open water, all across what was supposed to be the ice-locked North Pole. It was just messed up out there, like a battlefield, and it crossed my mind that we were flying out in a helicopter post-mission, looking down at the devastation and destruction left behind after a military encounter, just like those battlefields I have witnessed on many occasions.

Vic Vicary

1. Introduction

We need to tackle two crises at once. Whether we like it or not the world has changed, it looks completely different from how it did a few months ago and it will probably not look the same again, and we are going to have to choose a new way forward.

Greta Thunberg

This is the story of my part in an attempt by three British explorers to walk to the Geographic North Pole (GNP). It's a true story of an Arctic expedition, of a battle against the elements, and a classic tale of modern-day exploration, and yet it is so much more. It is not a story of huge successes – in fact, it's quite the opposite, which in some people's eyes could have been deemed a failure. I'll let the reader decide.

It's a book about leadership, planning and preparation, mental resilience, and coping with things that are out of our control. It may provoke discussion, provide you with some 'top tips', take-homes and lessons which may be of benefit to you in your world as you deal with whatever is thrown at you – things either within or outside your control. Speaking of things that seem outside of your control – of which there are many, including Covid-19 – our adventure into the Arctic tells the most important story of our time, a story of the effects of the global climate crisis.

Our Mission

It's a widely accepted fact that the ice caps are melting at an alarming rate. Climate scientists are now predicting that the Arctic could be effectively ice-free by 2058. These rapid environmental changes will likely consign epic, long range, polar ice expeditions to the pages of history.
Our mission was to document what we saw on ice.
The team's aim for the expedition was to capture the global significance of this remote region before it changed dramatically. The deteriorating conditions on the ice were to make this journey, quite literally, a 'Race Against Time'.
We were to infiltrate the frozen Arctic Ocean and report back on the current situation around the Geographic North Pole – was there a crisis?

So the most important focus of this book, and our story during the Race Against Time expedition, is a vivid illustration of how the clock is ticking on the climate crisis – because as we found out and soon realised, it is a crisis! Like many other people, I was sceptical about the environmental crisis and what it was all about before I departed for this expedition. Yet having seen the reality, having had my own plans hampered and curtailed by climate change, let me tell you, this is very real!

This book is part of my 'Battle Damage Assessment' (BDA – military terminology). It should be a wake-up call to every single one of us, however small and insignificant we think our contribution is, to be part of making a change and creating a difference for our future, the future for us and our children – my children! This is the real 'Race Against Time'.

Now, I'm not a climate scientist, but climate scientist Dr Stephan Harrison has kindly contributed to this book in chapter 8 to provide some context to what we had witnessed at the Pole.

I was busy finalising this book in the first half of 2020 when the world was suddenly faced by another crisis – the threat of the coronavirus, and all that this meant for people across the globe. Suddenly, many aspects of life that we had taken for granted, including our health, were under attack, and our 'normal' lives changed in many ways. Many of the lessons I have learnt, both in my service in the forces, and at the extremes of the planet, are applicable in any sort of crisis, as I hope that this book demonstrates. Endurance, patience, self-reliance, working with others, and adapting plans to new situations can all equally apply to many crises, such as the coronavirus pandemic, as much as it does to expeditions in the North and South Poles and to facing the climate crisis. This could be about reaching your very own 'North Pole'!

We can bury our heads in the sand for so long, but we just have to look around us: bushfires, bizarre weather fronts such as the 'Beast from the East', storms, floods, health disasters, including these pandemics, all bear witness to what the environment is telling us. This is happening globally and it should make us realise how 'fragile' we actually are.

> *I often talk to people who say, 'No, we have to be hopeful and to inspire each other, and we can't tell [people] too many negative things' … But, no –* **we have to tell it like it is**. *Because if there are no positive things to tell, then what should we do, should we spread false hope? We can't do that;* **we have to tell the truth**.
> Greta Thunberg TEDx Stockholm, December 2018

2. So, Who Am I?

*It's not getting to the top of the mountain or achieving some
great success, but often it's the journey it takes to get there...*
Vic Vicary

I went to the Geographic North Pole – but so what, why, and most importantly, why me? I wasn't one of the many eco-tourists or thrill-seekers trekking across the planet to justify my own personal means or glory. No, there's a little more to this story.

Firstly, I hate talking about myself. It makes me feel uncomfortable and I prefer to remain discreet about my background. However, I feel that I must tell you this story and at least a little something about myself, so that you understand a bit about who I am, some of my background and how I got into all of this. However, this is not a book primarily about me, it's about you and, hopefully, what we can all learn.

So, I was born in 1970, in Blackpool, one of three children to Eric and Beryl. My dad worked for the removals company *Pickford's* as a manager, and we moved down the country from my birth town, through Yorkshire and I eventually resided in Cornwall as a youth. I went to secondary school in Falmouth and was forever adventurous and, to be honest, a bit of a rogue.

I can always remember wanting to join the Army from an early age, and I had toy guns and uniforms acting out as a soldier, probably like most young boys. I went on adventures in the long grass with a compass and water bottle; unbeknown to me I was actually acting out my true destiny. Where that impulse came from, I'm not sure. Was it hereditary? Apparently, some ancestor had links to exploration and those famous words, "Dr Livingstone, I presume?" This may sound strange, and although this is something that I have not looked into, I do feel driven by someone or something that supports and protects me during the incredible experiences and journeys I have so far undertaken.

As a teenager growing up in Cornwall, I joined Falmouth Army Cadets as soon as I could, which luckily took me off the streets. I thoroughly enjoyed it, progressing to the dizzy rank of Lance Corporal! Aged 16, I left school with average qualifications (looking back, I'm sure I could have done better), but I did try my best! To my parents' surprise I went straight to the local careers office in Redruth to join up and I was sent off to the Army recruitment selection at Sutton Coldfield for my first ever journey by train to what was to be my destiny.

This was my first test, part of the Army recruitment selection process, where I thought that I was joining the Army Air Corps to fly helicopters! However, after passing all the tests, they sat me down and told me that if I wanted to join straight away, then it was to be in the Light Infantry, at a new leadership school, joining as a Junior Leader. This sounded great, so of course I jumped at it. I joined in 1986, the year (ironically) that Status Quo brought out 'In the Army Now' which often echoed down the corridors of our billets whilst we were cleaning our rooms for inspection. I followed the intensive leadership training at Sir John Moore Barracks, Winchester, for a year. Although I was determined and driven, I was also naïve and it was something of a wake-up call – teaching me how to shave (albeit only 'bum fluff'), iron my uniform, discipline myself, leadership and so much more. Humility aside, I was a born natural, sticking at it and putting up with everything thrown at me.

This was what I wanted to do, and I also earned my first pay packet for something I actually enjoyed! My parents were initially very proud but, of course, they started to worry when operational areas of conflict such as Ireland, Bosnia, Afghanistan, and Iraq came into my sight. Nevertheless, they were always pleased to see me. My father could never really understand why I wanted to subject myself to such dangers and trials, possibly because he had served in the RAF during the war.

After leaving Winchester in 1988, I joined my battalion, which was operational in Omagh, Northern Ireland, during the troubles. I was still so young, looking like a boy-soldier, and it was a tough unit given all that they had to face. It was a bit of a culture shock for me, transitioning into adulthood and joining a fully operational unit, although the Army training had prepared me well, in part. I did a variety of insignificant courses as, due to my age, (17 years) I wasn't fully allowed to be on the streets yet, which was frustrating for me.

One of those courses was a clerical course, which qualified me to become a Combat Company Clerk! To be honest, this was like being a receptionist for a boss, stuck in an office and churning out constant paperwork – at a time when we had typewriters! This really was something I did not want to do and I hated it, but I had been talked into it.

Even though I was working in a clerical role, I still went on the streets, manned the sangers and I sadly witnessed many impacts of the troubles. My unit and company sustained one of the worst atrocities of the conflict in 1988, when one of our coaches returning from the airport, full of soldiers coming back from leave, was blown to smithereens, killing eight friends and wounding 28 others.

After this, in 1990, the unit was sent to a 'happier' posting in Berlin. This was an exciting and interesting time for me. Sadly, I was still clerically based as I was actually doing a very good job. The Chief Clerk said that I could go all the way, but this was the last thing I wanted. I didn't join the Army to be a clerk, so my only way out was to underperform. This was unnatural for me, but I decided it was necessary in order to be a soldier. My underperformance was soon noticed and I was dragged in front of my boss to answer for my poor conduct. I explained that I just wanted to be a soldier! I was reprimanded and cross-posted to another company, but soon after I rose through the ranks, passing my career courses with merit and being quickly promoted – a route not to be recommended, but it worked!

In Berlin we were training for the Cold War and the fear of a Russian invasion. I vividly remember the Berlin Wall during the East–West divide, and then standing on it the day it came down. What an amazing and historic event to have experienced and witnessed.

After this two-year commitment, we were then sent to what is called a 'home posting'. We were a predominately Cornish unit and so were sent to Bulford near Salisbury, some four hours from Cornwall! I was made a Corporal, and I began to gain more and more experience, knowledge and skills: I took junior commanders' career courses, a jungle warfare course in Brunei, plus a six-month posting to Belize which, unbeknown to me, was to prepare me for what lay ahead.

Army days

Another two years, and time for another stint in Germany, this time training in armoured personnel carriers. These were vehicles I had seen as a young boy in the literature at the recruitment centre in Cornwall and had always wanted to drive. This time I was commanding (and sometimes driving) one. I had some interesting and fun times getting to know these vehicles and training with them across Germany and in Canada.

Whilst in Paderborn in Germany, I had attended a briefing from someone who had previously been in our unit and was now in a Specialist Military Unit (SMU). I was blown away. I thought back then, *That's what I want to do*. The seed had been sown. However, the timing wasn't right; I was married with young children and felt I could not commit to what I thought they were asking from me at the time.

After Germany, I conducted another tour of Northern Ireland, this time as a Team Leader, once again seeing more sides of the troubles. Soon after, I was posted out externally for a two-year stint in Catterick, North Yorkshire, to broaden my horizons as an Instructor at the Infantry Battle School. This taught young recruits the basics, which I found a little frustrating and uneventful.

Sadly, back in the UK my personal life took a bad turn and I ended up divorcing my wife. This was a devastating time for me and, looking back, it affected my mental health. Being away from my three young children broke my heart. Losing what felt like everything, I turned to unhealthy habits to cope, including alcohol. Luckily for me, someone tapped me on the shoulder one night in the mess and asked, "What are you doing, Vic?" This was the turning point.

I took a decisive step and started training, training, training. I wanted the chance to try out that specialist unit! I stopped drinking and started physical and psychological training, preparing myself for what would be, at the time, the hardest test of my life. I suppose things happen for a reason and we have these landmarks in our lives.

However, when I applied for the SMU, my unit was then posted to Bosnia for a six-month operational tour. I was forced to postpone selection and, although a setback, this did not deter me. In Bosnia I organised a very structured and progressive goal-setting approach to the whole process of selection (which I explain later on in chapter 4). Unbeknown to me, this programme set me up for success. I also started swotting up on the theory of what I expected to face, such as navigation, nutrition, the theory of physical training techniques and being in captivity; I read the standard stories about this unit to give me an understanding of what and who I was about to join. In fact, this put me on a good trajectory.

In Bosnia I had more of an intelligence role, visiting various locations and obtaining information about the current situation. This was interesting, but a distraction from what I really wanted to do! I spent a lot of time in the gym training hard progressively and sensibly with my own personal programme. I also built up my cardiovascular (CV) and endurance fitness with some great runs around the local area, training for what was the first mini goal I set myself – the 2000 London Marathon.

And so, on return to the UK, I ran the London Marathon, achieving what I had set out to do, in the time I had set myself. This enabled me to start building on my physical and psychological resilience, which was just the start of many other mini goals that I had set myself in order to reach my final goal. The rest was history and in July 2000, I was on the starting line, doing it for real. After many trials and tests, and a rigorous and arduous selection procedure, I was one of the lucky few who had successfully achieved my goal; but this was to be just the start....

And so, during the past 20 years, I've been to all of the nice places, having looked the enemy in the eye and having had a huge variety of

jobs. This provided me with a wealth of experience in a number of different fields, working to the values and ethos of the organisation and in return helping me get set up for life. I also managed to achieve a variety of qualifications, including: a Master's degree in Security and Risk Management; coaching and mentoring; leadership and management; health and safety; diversity and inclusion; and a teaching certificate, to name but a few. Alongside this, I progressed my advanced medical skills into becoming a paramedic, alongside qualifications in remote medicine and emergency and primary health care. I challenged myself academically, alongside my career, to prepare me for my eventual transition into the civilian world. With my extended medical knowledge and mountain skills, and through pushing my own resilience, I now have these hard and soft skills, helping others that may require my support – some of which you will read about throughout this book.

Ultimately, we're only human and I'm really not 'special' in any form. I've had to work hard to get to where I wanted to go and what I wanted to do. I've had to push myself into areas where I have been uncomfortable. Ultimately, you never know unless you give it a go, so it's worth taking those steps towards reaching your own goals.

3. The South Pole: The Seed of a Plan

Someone's sitting in the shade today because someone planted a tree a long time ago.

Warren Buffett

In the winter of 2011/2012, I was lucky to be part of a team (well, in fact two teams) that set out to recreate the historic Scott/Amundsen race to the Geographic South Pole. A Channel 4 news report on Christmas Day 2011 explained the rationale behind the trip:

A group of serving British soldiers are trekking across the Antarctic ice, following in the footsteps of explorers Captain Robert Falcon Scott and Norwegian Roald Amundsen as they duelled to reach the South Pole first 100 years ago.

It is the first time anyone has attempted to re-enact the race since the original expedition.

The soldiers have split into two teams – the Scott team and the Amundsen team – and are attempting to complete the most authentic ever modern-day recreation of the race. In doing so they hope to raise £500,000 for the Royal British Legion.

Both teams set off 53 days ago and have trekked over 400 nautical miles each so far. They are aiming to reach the South Pole in mid-January after 70 days of trekking, but could be delayed by the weather.

Lieutenant Colonel Henry Worsley leads the Amundsen team which is currently in front.

Worsley's team have a shorter distance to travel than the Scott team but have to cross more difficult terrain. It is believed they are the first team to cross the Axel Heiberg Glacier unsupported since Amundsen's original expedition.

By contrast, and following Captain Scott's original plan, the Scott team have to travel over 150 nautical miles extra, but their route takes them on much flatter terrain and around the Beardmore Glacier.

I was proud to be a member of the Scott team in an expedition which was under the overall command of Henry Worsley.

My First Expedition

In actual fact, my first foray into the expedition world had been in the Andes, in Peru, as part of some pre-training for a British military attempt on the Everest West Ridge in 2004. In addition to being a member of the team, I was also the expedition medic and had my work cut out, as well as learning a few lessons. One member of the team became ill up on the mountain with High Altitude Pulmonary Oedema (HAPE), so I had to treat him remotely, as well as CASEVAC (casualty evacuation) him safely – an event which could have been fatal. On the back of this I wrote a piece on altitude illness for a diploma in emergency and primary healthcare. The following extract explains what happened:

We stayed at our base camp (4,200m) for 24 hours with no problems but then had to ascend to start our ascent. Our objective was a mountain called 'Yanapaccha' (5460m) and our next bivvi site was to be at 4,800m. This would mean a climb of 600m with heavy kit (as donkeys cannot get up there). We left mid-afternoon (in the heat) with our heavy rucksacks and ascended some arduous country (across large grass and boulder fields). By the time we reached our bivvi site the majority of us were exhausted. We all fed on freeze-dried rations and tried to sleep in preparation for our attempt at the summit at 4am. To say that none of our team slept at 4,800m was an understatement. It was a very disturbed sleep for all of us. (This should have set the alarm bells ringing!)

Climbing Piscu in Peru

At 4am we reveilled, had a quick brew and prepared ourselves for our summit attempt. One of our team (my climbing partner) was not very well and had signs of AMS (acute mountain sickness). He also had some classic symptoms of HAPE. In particular, he was coughing (bent over) and was only comfortable sitting up. The team leader was informed and a CASEVAC was arranged. The casualty was taken down the mountain in the dark accompanied by myself, a 'guide' at the front and an additional two climbers (in case the casualty became a stretcher case). This was ideal and meant a fast descent via the best route. The remainder of the team waited until first light and decided to abandon their summit attempt.

The casualty was taken back down to 4,200m (taking two hours) and rested back in his tent where I looked after him. After about two hours we decided to CASEVAC the *casualty back to Huaraz to see a doctor. During this time, I was looking after him and the team leader was informing (via satphone) our doctor back home. This was useful, especially for any other recommendations. The casualty greatly improved during descent and was fully stable back in Huaraz (where he remained during the rest of the expedition). This was a lesson to be learnt and from then on, we approached our climbs more cautiously with more rest time prior to and after each ascent.*

The expedition was a challenge, what with the weights we were carrying and the altitudes we were rapidly ascending – probably too fast. We experienced some 'summit fever', a compulsion by the team leader to reach the summit of the mountain at all costs (or that is what it felt like, at least). So the leader (who later struggled himself) was challenged to abort the attempt of one of the mountains, based on the medical advice that I was giving. We were not strictly going by the book, carrying huge weights and travelling too fast at such a high altitude which, of course, led to altitude sickness. If you cut corners in areas of altitude, or in fact in any expedition, there is a high risk of fatalities.

Unfortunately, due to my squadron being operational at the time and the current world situation, I had to return to the UK, sadly missing the chance to be selected for the Army 2005 Everest West Ridge expedition. Instead, I had to travel out to an operational theatre and do my full-time job.

Nevertheless, this expedition training had been an eye-opener in a number of ways, providing me with the role of expedition medic, experiencing the extra kit we had to carry, as well as the added responsibility, pressure, and the remoteness of the work involved. It was something I actually enjoyed. I learnt a lot of lessons which I put into my operational work role and expeditions. It didn't put me off – if anything it made me more determined. It put another layer on top of my own resiliency, a bit like adding another layer of Kevlar to your own body armour.

Tempted to the Pole

In 2008, as part of a yearly briefing at work where we learnt from various endeavours and operations, Mark Langridge (ML) gave a briefing about his solo attempt at the Geographic South Pole. This intrigued me so much that I expressed a desire to do the same when he asked for volunteers to do something else.

Mark had followed a well-trodden route favoured by soloists and those wanting to break records going from Hercules Inlet to the Geographic South Pole (GSP). To make it more challenging, Mark had planned to go to the GSP and back again, but unfortunately, whilst approaching the pole, he realised he wouldn't be able to make it back, and so aborted the return leg, following Shackleton's adage of "better a live donkey than a dead lion!"

On the back of this, Mark explained that in the winter of 2011/2012 they were looking at attempting a centenary race to the South Pole following in the footsteps of Amundsen and Scott. Straight away I told him to put my name down!

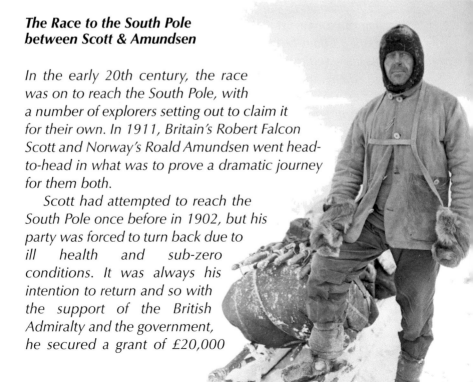

The Race to the South Pole between Scott & Amundsen

In the early 20th century, the race was on to reach the South Pole, with a number of explorers setting out to claim it for their own. In 1911, Britain's Robert Falcon Scott and Norway's Roald Amundsen went head-to-head in what was to prove a dramatic journey for them both.

Scott had attempted to reach the South Pole once before in 1902, but his party was forced to turn back due to ill health and sub-zero conditions. It was always his intention to return and so with the support of the British Admiralty and the government, he secured a grant of £20,000 and recruited men from his original Antarctic voyage and also from Ernest Shackleton's ship Nimrod, recently returned from the Antarctic. The crew of the Terra Nova included naval seamen, scientists and paying members, and they sailed from Cardiff on 15th June 1910.

Roald Amundsen was a respected Norwegian explorer who was determined to beat the British and be the first to reach the South Pole. He kept his plans to head south very secret – in fact, he had originally planned to head north, but upon hearing that the North Pole had been reached, changed his mission.

Amundsen's ship, the Fram, reached the Ross Ice Shelf on 14th January 1911, Amundsen having chosen to land at the Bay of Whales. This gained the Norwegians a 60-mile advantage over Scott, who landed at McMurdo Sound.

On 18th October 1911, after the Antarctic winter, Amundsen's team set out on its drive toward the Pole. Captain Scott began his trek three weeks later. At around 1500 hours on 14th December 1911, Amundsen raised the flag of Norway at the South Pole. He had reached the Pole a full 33 days before Captain Scott arrived. Amundsen and his crew returned to their base camp on 25th January 1912, 99 days and roughly 1400 nautical miles after their departure.

Scott left his base camp with his team to the Pole on 1st November 1911. He finally reached the South Pole on 17th January 1912, disappointed to learn that Amundsen had beaten him to it. The tortuous return journey was faced with stoicism and dignity. Weak from exhaustion, hunger and extreme cold, his last diary entry is dated 29th March 1912. He died in his tent alongside two of his men.

Amundsen's success was celebrated worldwide, and he received personal telegrams of congratulations from US President Theodore Roosevelt and King George V of England. Scott was also recognised for his achievements and posthumously made a Knight Commander of the Order of the Bath.

Later, Henry Worsley and ML gave a presentation about the intended expedition, inviting all those who were interested. Amongst two handfuls of other people, I was there as they talked about their accomplishments and ambitions. I thought this was going to be 'Mission: Impossible'! Captain RF Scott had walked to the Pole with ponies and tractors, and sadly after turning home had perished – almost within shouting distance of safety. The Norwegians, led by Roald Amundson, had successfully completed the journey using dogs, although they never man-hauled all the way with all of their supplies. What Henry and Mark were attempting, to re-enact the same routes whilst man-handling our loads all the way (which in theory made it fairer, although Team Scott would have 920 statute miles to cover compared to Team Amundsen's 800), had never been done before, let alone 100 years to the day of the historic expedition. This was what we intended to accomplish!

I like a challenge, and so I thought, *Let's go.* I had a desire to go on an adventure, to do an expedition of this kind. It felt right, as though it was meant to be. Apparently, my own family forefathers were explorers, and I have always felt a desire for adventure and challenge since my early childhood. Whilst this might sound crazy, I put it down to a 'sixth-sense', a feeling that someone is always with me, pushing me and dragging me to do these things, whilst always protecting me. I felt it was my destiny!

I've had this feeling on a few occasions, and I've also had a few near-death experiences and wondered how on earth I survived, particularly during my military career. One particular moment was on operations where I received an enormous burst of gun fire landing around my feet. I took cover behind a huge rock, only to hear the massive weight of gunfire – that was a close one!

The trip would cost £5K per person, thus demonstrating commitment from each participant to stump up the cash required. (In the end I took out a loan to cover the cost.) Eventually, they put all the names of those eager to take part in a hat and drew out the 'lucky' few. By the way, prior to the selection I had taken my wife to the pub and told her about the expedition over a candle-lit dinner! I explained to her how I had a strong feeling that I was going on the trip; I just knew. When it came to it, I was asked to pull the names out of the hat – and I pulled out a piece of paper with my own name on it. Destiny!

Training

We all managed to get away for a week and come together, as due to our operational backgrounds everyone had been spread across the globe. With a total of six people (some had to eventually drop out due to operational commitments, so some reserves substituted for them) we travelled to Norway for a week's training. It was to be a week on a ginormous frozen lake, approximately 20km long. We had stopped off overnight with our Norwegian military counterparts who supported us with accommodation, rations and fuel – a great bunch of guys. We prepared our kit there and did some training. I gave a lesson about moving on ice, roping up, and walking with a pulk (sledge), based on my mountain troop experience. The next day we moved onto the lake, enabling us to progressively get used to our kit and mould together as a team, setting up our tents and overnighting.

Norway training

One of the biggest shocks were our boots – they were cold, ill-fitting and felt like cardboard, and it wasn't just because we were breaking them in. They were awful! Our feet were that bad that eventually, the following day, we decided to turn around and call it a day. It wasn't until the sun went down and we had another taste of the extreme cold that we started to feel it and struggle. What a start and shock that was! There were also a couple of guys who struggled and were not properly prepared nutritionally. But it was training, we could take it in stages. Thankfully, that's exactly what we did.

At the end, after making it back to our refuge – the minibus – we sat freezing and licking our wounds, realising what we had taken on, with the reality of what lay ahead gradually dawning on all of us. This was a baptism of fire, but it proved the worth of training and preparation, and a necessary shock. A good job it wasn't the real thing!

In Oslo we bought ourselves a really good pair of boots. Alfa boots are a credible polar brand and well known for their value in expeditions such as this. We also bought four pairs of socks: a thin pair, a liner (a waterproof bag), a thick pair of socks, and then the inside boot (which has a liner that moulds to your foot and is made of reindeer fur). All of this sits inside a Gor Tex Gaitor boot. All-in-all £400 worth of footwear, but money well invested. As the old adage goes, 'Buy cheap, buy twice', and this we could not afford whilst on expedition.

It was a good job we did that, as we would have failed with the boots we initially wore. However, this is the point of any training – to identify any lessons that need to be learnt. The sales assistant laughed at the boots we were going to use, emphasising to us how it is foolish to cut corners on kit in a polar region. He must have wondered, *Who are these British novice idiots?!* The superior items may come at an expense, but that's the way it is. After all, once you're out there, you're on your own.

To prepare for the South Pole we undertook further training. I was the only guy on the team with mountain experience, so I taught the others some rope skills, especially how to use the pulk's harnesses to rescue each other if anyone fell into a crevasse, and how the pulk would lock if you fell. We had team and individual meetings, kit issue and kit preparation.

We also took part in various meetings to get to know each other and to raise the profile of the expedition. We performed a stunt off the Lloyds building in the City of London, abseiling from the roof with our pulks and, you guessed it, I had to do all the rope work, which was in fact quite a stressful experience making sure it was all safe, particularly in front of the general public and the media. The event was publicised in the *Metro* newspaper, raising awareness as well as money. Luckily it all went smoothly!

At the time that the Antarctic expedition was due to begin, I considered myself to be extremely fit. After all, as part of my job I was leading young students across the Brecon Beacons for navigation and fitness training. This was pretty tough, particularly when they were all younger than me, and I was the role model and leader. However, I was conscious that I carried no fat on me (I couldn't afford to), and so I worried that I was going to struggle as I felt the cold at the Pole. I remember that before we left, I had gone out to walk the dog in the UK on a cold, wet and horrible morning in October. I came back home absolutely freezing and thought to myself, *God, if I'm cold here, then I need to sort myself out for the South Pole!* Nevertheless, I was otherwise fit, both mentally and physically (or as fit as I could be). I had to prepare as I had done before, utilising the same goal-setting techniques and a holistic approach to understanding the environment both physically and mentally, something I will discuss later.

Health challenge

In 2011, I received some devastating news that I had been diagnosed with a serious medical condition called TRAPS, an extremely rare DNA disorder where the individual cannot sufficiently control their inflammatory levels. I believe that I am the only person in the world now living with my specific genetic disorder. Great, I am a mutant! To be honest, although the news was disturbing, it was actually a relief to finally have a diagnosis and know what I had, as after five years of investigations, I had become drained and exhausted not only with the visits to doctors but also with having to manage the pain and associated fevers. I was reaching the psychological limits of the illness for myself and my family as well.

TRAPS: The following includes two excerpts from a paper written by my consultant, about me, for a prestigious medical journal!

Abseiling off the Lloyds building with Henry Worsley

TNF receptor associated periodic syndrome (TRAPS) is an autosomal dominant disease caused by gain-of-function mutations in the TNF superfamily receptor 1A (TNFRSF1A) gene encoding 55 kDa TNF receptor type I (TNFR1). TRAPS was initially described in 1982 in an Irish-Scottish family with a 'periodic disease' complicated by AA amyloidosis. Subsequently it has been reported in ethnic groups including Caucasians, Black Americans, Japanese and subjects of Mediterranean ancestry. The disease is characterized by episodes of fever accompanied by severe abdominal pain, arthralgia, myalgia, rash, chest pain, lymphadenopathy and red, swollen eyes. The duration of the attacks can range from few days to several weeks, with the onset from early childhood to adulthood. During febrile episodes patients with TRAPS demonstrate elevation of C-reactive protein (CRP) and serum amyloid A (SAA) protein and without effective treatment these patients are at high risk of developing AA amyloidosis.

Case Report

A 41 year old British man from non-consanguineous kindred was referred to our clinic by an infectious diseases unit with a history of recurrent fevers. He had presented immediately after a period working in Asia and an extensive work up had demonstrated persistent inflammatory disease but no underlying infectious or autoimmune cause. On direct questioning he described previously undisclosed symptoms from early adolescence with an appendectomy at the age of 12. Since then he had had 10 to 12 attacks of severe abdominal pain per year. These lasted almost exactly two weeks usually starting in either loin and moved to the front of his abdomen. Other attack features included pleuritic chest pain, headache, arthralgia, myalgia, night sweats, generalised erythema and unilateral painless cervical lymphadenopathy. He had occasional red eyes but no periorbital oedema or periorbital pain. He was of normal population height but significantly shorter than his siblings and had a late onset of puberty at 16 years of age. He thought his attacks might be triggered by stress, cold, physical exercise and in some cases diet. He was physically extremely fit and in full time employment having never had any time off his work for his attacks. He has never been on any medication. On examination he had bilateral red eyes and a generalised erythematous rash particularly across his chest. He was tender over his left loin with no features of peritonism nor evidence of arthritis. He had minor cervical lymphadenopathy. His inflammatory markers were elevated: SAA 258 mg/L and CRP 87 mg/L. His three siblings, parents and four children all denied any similar symptoms. His clinical picture was thought to be consistent with TRAPS and genetic testing was performed.

Further testing and bi-annual check-ups continue to this day. I was diagnosed with a rare genetic disorder which is actually very serious if left untreated. I had been continuing thinking it was normal, but it was steadily grinding me down and becoming unbearable with the associated symptoms. I had become like a bear with a sore head and, looking back, would never want to go back to how I was at that time. I'm not sure how I coped but somehow, I did.

So, what impact does this have on my life? Firstly, I have to inject myself daily with a drug called anakinra to control my inflammatory levels. The problem with this is not just the injecting, but also managing the medicine itself when I'm out doing wild expeditions. The drug is to be kept 'fridge cold' and is not allowed to be frozen or shaken because it is 'live', otherwise the medication could be damaged, or even destroyed, thus rendering it useless. Which believe me is a difficult requirement when out in the field!! There is also the extra weight of carrying the medication which has to be placed in a special box to prevent it from freezing and protect it from being shaken, a difficult ask when it's in my pulk and I'm dragging it over ice boulder fields, for example. In addition, I have to undergo regular check-ups in London to make sure I'm okay.

Injecting in Antarctica, the 'magic box' and my injection itself

So what? Well, I have to live with this condition and manage it myself. There are many other people living with illnesses much worse than mine, and I am grateful to still be fit and healthy and able to do what I set out to achieve. For example, having diabetes might seem to be just a matter of managing sugar levels. I'm sure this is easier said than done, but it does not prevent or restrict diabetic people from doing something out of the norm. An expedition to the Poles, climbing Everest or something else is still within reach – the condition just needs to be managed properly.

However, I had to persuade my consultant to let me take these trips, and after a heated argument he soon realised that I would not be held back by my illness. Back in 2011 when setting off to the South Pole, he tried to stop me with worries about the drugs and how I would manage. I reassured him and ultimately said that I was going anyway!

I did not actually divulge this condition to the team until we were at the leaving party in London. The guys were not too fussed and said that it was my problem to deal with, as long as I carried my own medication, which I rightfully did (at an extra weight of approximately 6kg). I actually

Training in Germany

plucked up the courage to tell Henry when we were on the flight to Chile as I was going into the toilet on the aircraft. I showed him the medication I was about to inject and explained my situation. Needless to say, he wasn't too impressed but, to be honest, there wasn't much he could do either at this late stage!

Heading South

The actual South Pole expedition was, in theory, three months long. We would fly from London to Chile and stay in the southernmost town of the country called Punta Arenas. Next, we would fly to a 'patrol' base set up by the Antarctic Logistics & Expeditions (ALE), stay there and do some pre-training. Finally, we would be dropped off by a special plane to land on the ice. How many times in life, and especially in the military, would you spend 76 days 'living in the field', sharing a tent with two other people in a remote place?

The key to any long expedition is travelling during the right season and having a good and early start. A century earlier, Scott and Amundsen had gone to the Antarctic by ship, set up camp, built cabins and lived there. Some of their team members signed up for years on end, with no hope of seeing home for several years if not longer. Modern exploration is not like that; significant trips are compressed into short time-spans, trying to take advantage of the best weather and light conditions, as well as working with constraints imposed by the logistics companies. Perhaps it has not actually changed for the best!

There are two seasons in the South Pole – total darkness and total daylight. For safety reasons, logistics companies facilitate your travel to and from the Pole. They will drop you off, but if you don't get there in time, they will pick you up and take you home. It is all very seasonal, and so expeditions, particularly long-haul ones, are under huge pressure to get out first and complete their plans in time, otherwise there can be serious safety concerns and possible failure. The Antarctic Logistics & Expeditions (ALE) was a professional and helpful outfit, and following their advice was important to avoid endangering yourselves, others in the region, and members of the ALE trying to help you. This is a huge and important decision to bear in mind, as having to be picked up in an emergency due to your own foolhardiness would result in potential fatalities as well as huge embarrassment.

When we arrived in Punta Arenas there were no forward flights available to the camp at Union Glacier. Annoyingly, I picked up a cold and didn't feel very well. This could have also been linked to having a low immune system as a result of my diagnosed illness, added to the fact that I would have been run down from arduous training at work. However, whilst we waited, we prepared our equipment and re-packaged all our food ready for the expedition. We also managed to try all the local restaurants, drink Chilean wine (which I love) and eat all the food, done in a deliberate attempt to help me put on as much weight as possible! We were stuck there for two weeks due to poor weather conditions (which is actually not uncommon) but, luckily, we had prepared ourselves and all of our kit, and recovered from our colds.

Extracts from my diary give real-time insight into the expedition and what we were experiencing. Interestingly, my wife, heavily pregnant at the time, also kept a diary. Her account provides a fascinating insight into the pressures experienced by those we love and leave behind. The crucial support team for any expedition is those we love.

Wednesday 19th October 2011
I awoke with a serious sore throat, not good – this means a cold. I must have picked it up due to jetlag and going from hot / cold environments, plus the guys have got one – great! Just what I needed!

Saturday 29th October 2011
We were off, and met the Iluysian aircraft, a monstrosity of a Russian plane made in the 70s. Winds were very strong as we got onto the plane. A little wait and the engines started with a roar, such power! We were leaving Punta, next stop Antarctica.
*   Union Glacier! Landed! -23°C, -38°C windchill on airstrip. V. cold!! A bit of a shock to the system. 70 days of this – what a wake-up call. Definitely a shock to the system.*

As soon as we reached Antarctica and got off the plane, Antarctic shock set in! The temperature was -40 degrees – the cold was just horrific and a huge shock if you have not been exposed to these temperatures previously. We set up our tents and thankfully ALE looked after us well because they had an established facility complete with great quality hot food.

Once acclimatised, we received another shock whilst doing some training – the amount of weight that we had to pull! We were all in the same boat, each with 160kg on the pulk (equivalent to the weight of two men). One guy was very shocked and pulled out on day one, but to be honest he had done little preparatory training and looked unwell. As expedition leader, Henry Worsley had been aware of his condition. In his defence, some years later the same man suffered a heart attack which he thankfully survived.

> <u>Sunday 30th October 2011</u> *(whilst still at camp)*
> *We decided to pull our pulks with the full weight less the tent, tent bags, sleeping bags. Must be about 160kg! V. heavy and hard-going pulling. We went out for about an hour, doing 15 minutes each. The weather changed so many times throughout and meant stopping and adjusting our kit, wiping our goggles. One minute we were sweating, next minute we were cold. So variable and you need a change of hats, balaclavas, goggles, gloves etc. We went back after about 2½ hours in a sweat. A wake-up call for what is to come, but it seems achievable?!*

Extract from my wife's diary:

> <u>Sunday 30th October 2011</u>
> *You texted yesterday afternoon to confirm that ALE was finally able to fly you out to Union Glacier. Suddenly the reality of your venture is becoming very imminent and it scares me sick to think of what lies ahead of you.*

The Race Begins

We spent a week at the base before a flight became available. We then loaded up our pulks, ready to go. Team Amundsen was dropped off as close as possible to the Bay of Whales, the site of Amundsen's camp all those years ago.

The logistics company used Kenn Borek Air, essentially a taxi-fleet flown by some amazing Canadian 'hillbillies', but they had to locate fuel dumps dotted around Antarctica. Unlike your normal petrol service station, these locations are marked by flags in the ground. Once found, we had to dig the barrels out of the snow and pump the fuel out, creating a right sweat before we had even started trekking (the pilots were not going to do it for us!).

We could see a look of shock and fear on the faces of Team Amundsen (especially in the face of the one guy who pulled out). As Team Scott, we were dropped on ice 1km short of Captain Scott's hut in the Bay of Whales. The pilot landed, jumped out and used his drill piece

Fuel stop in Antarctica – digging out the fuel

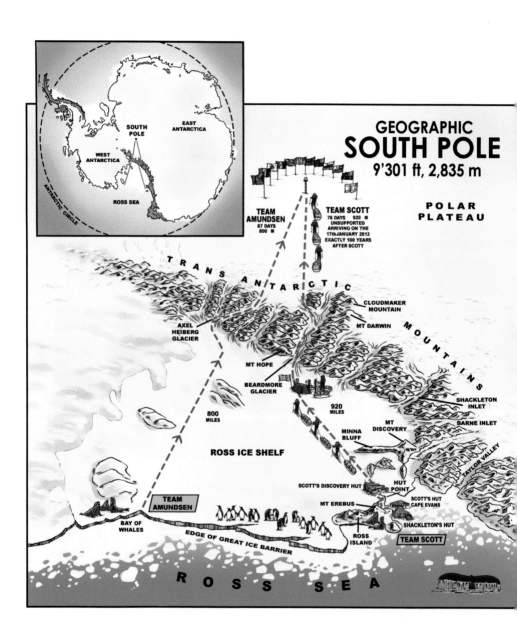

GEOGRAPHIC
SOUTH POLE
9'301 ft, 2,835 m

SOUTH
POLE

EAST
ANTARCTICA

WEST
ANTARCTICA

ROSS SEA

ANTARCTIC CIRCLE

POLAR
PLATEAU

TEAM
AMUNDSEN
67 DAYS
800 M

TEAM SCOTT
76 DAYS   920 M
UNSUPPORTED
ARRIVING ON THE
17th JANUARY 2012
EXACTLY 100 YEARS
AFTER SCOTT

T R A N S   A N T A R C T I C

M O U N T A I N S

CLOUDMAKER
MOUNTAIN

MT DARWIN

AXEL
HEIBERG
GLACIER

MT HOPE

BEARDMORE
GLACIER

920
MILES

SHACKLETON
INLET

BARNE INLET

800
MILES

MT
DISCOVERY

MINNA
BLUFF

TAYLOR VALLEY

ROSS ICE SHELF

SCOTT'S DISCOVERY HUT

HUT
POINT

TEAM
AMUNDSEN

MT EREBUS

SCOTT'S HUT
CAPE EVANS

SHACKLETON'S HUT

BAY OF
WHALES

EDGE OF GREAT ICE BARRIER

ROSS
ISLAND

TEAM SCOTT

R O S S   S E A

30

Outside Scott's Hut

The weather survey station at Scott's Hut

to check the thickness of ice. With the thumbs up, he threw our pulks off the plane onto good flat snow, and we skied to Captain Scott's hut where we set up our tents. As something of a Scott fanatic, this experience was like Christmas for me. It was totally amazing to be at Scott's hut, a century on, and as I soaked up the experience we walked around the site and took photos of the best campsite in the world! It was a piece of history which we had all read about, and it was a truly amazing opportunity that very few people ever get.

<u>*Wednesday 2nd November 2011*</u>
Departing VG Day 1
Well, this is it, the big day we have been waiting for! It's taken us nearly 2½ wks to get here. The plan is early reveille, and ready to go by 1000hrs. Slight delays, but we got underway. We said our farewells and left via a Dakota DC3; 2½ hrs later we were at our fuel replenishment site and dug the fuel out for the plane; 30 mins later we were on our way to drop off Amundsen Team. A parting farewell, sad but happy to see them go – this is it! Their ground looked good and the weather fair, but nothing in sight. It was like a snow desert.

Not long and we were on our way via our replen site. We had a scenic and enjoyable tour of the ground, seeing

Mount Erebus, Scott's hut, Shackleton's hut and McMurdo Sound. Unbelievable that what we have read about is now becoming real. 100 years to the day, we are v. excited about the thought and won't it be great to get to Scott's hut tonight?!

We went to the replen, a few dodgy attempts at landing and we were there. The fuel was still there some 8 years later. However, Jim the pilot decided to go for it and drop us at our start point – Cape Evans! What a result and what a good bloke. We said our farewells, having been dropped off, and me, Kev and Mark were the only people here!! We pulled our pulks towards Scott's hut – how surreal! Weather was good, although slightly windy but mild at the coast. This must be one of the world's greatest campsites. once-in-a-lifetime

Extract from my wife's diary:

<u>*Wednesday 2nd November 2011*</u>
One hundred years ago Scott and his men set off on their tragic journey. You and the other men are still at Union Glacier, but flying out tomorrow to your starting point. I wish you all the best of luck my love. I'm with you every step and I'm worried sick about the possible complications, with your medication, the bad storms/winds and general exhaustion in these freezing temperatures. Whilst I fully comprehend why you want to be part of this historic, once in a lifetime event, I struggle to get enthusiastic. I miss you so much and I feel weak and weepy.

The ice was all flat, and we had half a day there – what should we do? We decided that we had better get going; we only had 1,200 miles to go! The team was quite jolly plodding off, taking photos and chatting away, but the weight we had to pull was horrendous. Then we made it around the corner and, oh my God, the terrain was so hilly it was like the Alps. It was tough pulling the pulks uphill but also, when we went downhill they flew down toward us at such high speed. We did that for about six hours and we were exhausted. I thought to myself, *Oh my*

God, what is this all about? The actual realisation of this huge epic expedition had hit us in the face – but we had to just get on with it! I think we were all like that, feeling excited but also apprehensive about what lay ahead.

The second day, we continued for another seven hours and then set up tent in a place called McMurdo Sound, still near civilisation. It had an Antarctic base called the Discovery Hut, built by Scott in 1902 during the Discovery Expedition of 1901–1904, which we visited, being carefully watched by a few giant seals. Then we heard that the guy I previously mentioned from Team Amundsen had been pulled out by the flight as it returned from dropping us off. The fact that he dropped out was all a bit of a shock for us.

One key element of the expedition was that, because we were re-enacting a race, we were not to communicate with each other across teams (even though

Inside Scott's Discovery Hut

Scott had never conceived his expedition to be a race at the time, and for a long while thought that the prize of reaching the Pole first was his until he discovered the Norwegians' plans). As a result of having no contact with the other team, we were always wondering how they were progressing, but we just got on with the task. Team A had to do 800 miles through the steep Axel Heiberg Glacier, even though theirs was a shorter distance in total mileage. Our team had to go around that and through the Beardmore Glacier, giving us more distance (and we still had 10,000 ft to climb to get to the South Pole).

When the race was on, we never spoke to Team A at all. It had indeed become a proper race. We took with us Captain Lawrence Oates' Polar Medal (loaned to us from the Dragoons) which had been given to Lawrence posthumously. Oates, the only member of the expedition from the Army, had been the man in Scott's party who famously said, "I am just going outside and may be some time", in all probability sacrificing himself in the hope that the remaining party could save themselves without the extra burden of caring for and carrying a wounded and sick team member. It was a huge honour and privilege to be carrying Lawrence Oates' medal, we just had to get it to the Pole!

Memorialising Captain Lawrence Oates's polar medal, at the place where we believe he gave his life

'Seal Camp'
We arrived at Hut Point and our base was at the foot of Vince's Cross. Camp was erected more swiftly and routine is getting better. I'm melt man tonight. We put our sponsorship jackets on and made our way around the corner to Discovery Hut. Luckily, a party led by a guide was there and obviously very interested in us. We got Captain Oates' medal and that caused a stir. Afterwards, we sought refuge in our tent, where two seals were also sharing our site. The seals don't seem to care less and just lie there asleep (very large).

Pushing Across the Ice

Anyway, we plodded on, facing horrific weather, deep crevasses, mazes of rifts, and pretty extreme conditions, literally tracing the same footsteps as Captain Scott and his team. The amazing thing was that having read his diary, particularly the night before we were to face what we did, it was exactly as he wrote about. This was bizarre! It truly was untouched ground through which very few people have managed to trek. Captain Scott's diary was a godsend to us, and we actually felt he and his team were there with us at times – a feeling that was sometimes very eerie.

I have a little secret that is still a mystery to me and which I did not document in my diary. One night when I was lying in the tent getting ready to go to sleep, I vividly remember seeing Captain Scott's face in the wrinkles of the tent above me, looking down at me. It was very bizarre and I lay there just looking at it. Perhaps I was tired and hallucinating, as weird emotions and events took place out there, psychologically. However, every day thereafter, I looked up at that tent roof to try and find Scott again, but he never reappeared. I personally felt that Captain Scott was with us on our journey.

During the first month, we had a lot of thoughts in our minds and we could have probably survived on our own thoughts for a month quite well. Eventually, however, when your thoughts leave you a little, you start focusing on the pain and hardships and dangerously cling on to those thoughts instead. Therefore, I put into action the clever use of mental coping strategies which I used to teach to my 'hill' students,

What Scott saw in 1911

What we saw in 2011

37

including the use of distraction thoughts and drifting the mind to better places. Captain Scott also used these techniques and mentioned them in his diary, so it's nothing new! On Friday 29th December 1911 Scott wrote:

> *The marches are terribly monotonous. One's thoughts wander occasionally to pleasanter scenes and places, but the necessity to keep the course, or some hitch in the surface quickly brings them back.*

We would stop every hour, have nutrition, take a drink (all of which were critical), and during that first month we would talk to each other. However, in time, we simply nodded at each other, and would only talk in the tent at the end of the day whilst we were smoking our pipes. In the evening we would physically and mentally prepare for the next day, and then do it all again. This was mentally draining.

Planning our route

<u>Monday 7th November 2011</u>
A long hard trek today manhauling. It was difficult and after 6 hrs, was enough. The going was hard with hard crusty snow making it easier, then all of a sudden hitting sandy snow, which is like dragging a body uphill. It seems like we were going uphill all the time! My iPod gave in after 40 minutes and I was left to the sounds and sights of Antarctica, the pole hitting the ground, followed by the jet sound of dragging the pulk. 1 hour each x 2 = 6 hours, v. hard, and we need to push it more later (not yet), hopefully reaching 8–9 hours. The weather didn't help either, it was on or off hot with strong wind, so it meant constant changing of our gear.

<u>Wednesday 9th November 2011</u>
One cannot describe how hard it is! This is much harder than selection and is purely a test of man, I take my hat off to Capt Scott!

The snow is the usual soft and sandy making it extremely difficult. It felt like the devil was on my pulk!!

<u>Thursday 10th November 2011</u>
It was again hard work today, but I am becoming numb to the mental and physical rigours of manhauling. I managed to get 4 hrs of iPod towards the end which motivated me again, taking my mind off things. But one's mind wanders all over the place, whilst manhauling.

<u>Sunday 13th November 2011</u>
Well, today has been an awful day really. Firstly, I pulled a muscle in my back, but nothing too serious that a dose of Ibuprofen won't sort out. We were away by 0900 hrs, me leading and we were still in Nina's grasp [Nina Bluff]. She had laid a web of many crevasses through which we had to weave ourselves. Slight bit of wind, bright and sunny, ideal marching conditions really. Kev's pulk fell in a crevasse, like mine the other day, and I helped him get it out. Some of the

crevasses more hairline and then some grew very large, a bit worrying really.

After about 3 hrs of this we thought we had beaten her, but the wind grew much stronger again from the south and we were led into deep sastrugi, which was back-breaking (especially with my back!). The wind grew stronger and it sapped all our strength and after 5 hrs we called it a day. The windiest day so far putting the tent up, and we were so glad to warm up inside.

Extract from my wife's diary:

<u>Saturday 19th November 2011</u>
Today's audio report on the website displayed a first sign of onsetting tiredness. You've been on the 'road' for 18 days now of which only one day has been a 'rest' day due to bad weather. As silly as it sounds, I hope you'll get a snow storm to force you to stay in the tent for a day or two to give you some opportunity to rest!

Of course, we had some emotional days and rare instances of conflict, and we nearly came to fisticuffs a few times, as you would expect on any expedition. Emotions hit all of us, especially for Kev who had three little kids at the time. At one stage Kev had really red eyes, and when we asked if he was ok, he simply said that the wind was getting in his goggles. After the expedition he admitted that he had been thinking about his children, which I couldn't fully relate to at the time, although later, during the North Pole expedition, I knew exactly what he meant. Admittedly, I too had some 'eye-watering' days, as anyone would in a remote and isolated situation which can play havoc on your emotions.

Extracts from my wife's diary:

<u>Friday 2nd December 2011</u>
The other worry is the distance you still have to cover. Whilst you are doing very well and keep going, there are still over 400 miles ahead of you! You'll have to do an average of 13– 15 miles a day to finish by mid-Jan! I know you can do it,

there's no doubt and I'm very proud of you. It's just completely wrong timing, when I need you here.

Friday 2nd December 2011
The baby is fine, it's moving and kicking and seems unaware of all this kafuffle. I'm so excited about holding our own 'expedition baby' in our arms. Really can't wait to see what we're having!

Monday 5th December 2011
At least you sounded better today. I was a little worried about you yesterday as you sounded quite disheartened and tired. Morale is high, which is really important. I'm thinking of you 24/7 my love.

Returning to my diary:

Wednesday 7th December 2011
Another white out!
Awoke to a cold, overcast and dreary day outside. We packed up as normal, but the cloud and snow started to close in, to create our worst white out yet! I travelled 500m and we decided to call it a day, we really could not go on. Tent went up and got in, still quite mild when the snow flows*. Unfortunately, we knew that conditions don't get any better after a blizzard and can take 2–3 days to improve. Hopefully not.

Well, we made some phone calls, sewing and admin occupying ourselves. Actually, we should see this as a good day and nice rest!

By the way, 100 yrs to the day Scott was also stuck in a 4-day blizzard! How bizarre, eh? Still, there is not much we can do about this, we must sit this one out.

Thursday 8th December 2011
Utterly miserable.
Awoke to a windy tent, and a dull and wet day. It had cleared slightly, with a little sun and a little horizon (for

navigation). The decision was to go or not, which incurred a slight delay, before we thought we'd give it a go....

I led first (I always do) and the conditions were hard, like dragging the pulk on our first days laden with 160 kg! Navigation was difficult and the sun went in and out so I could use the shadow every so often. My main navigation aid was the southern wind, which poured soft spin drift towards me, so I knew it was south!

Anyway, we persevered and the wind was horrendously strong (balaclava on all day!), but the going became difficult and so did the weather! So, after 7 hrs of hard, utterly miserable marching we called it a day.

We tried to make light of a lot of the pressures, saying to each other that we would have fun things to send back to the website. Humour was a key way to help us survive, but we did have some very dark days,

The sketch of Beardmore Glacier from my diary

especially on the Beardmore Glacier, where we were stranded for four days over Christmas due to the weather. Stuck on that ledge we felt claustrophobic and we referred to it as 'Old Man Beardmore', fearing that this glacier was holding us there. We had such a sense of relief as soon as we were able to move on. I wrote in my diary:

Wednesday 14th December 2011
I had a bit of a blue moment towards the end of a good day, slightly emotional. I think it gets to you out here a lot more, but better now. This was due to a slight disagreement with Kev, which has been brewing for some time I feel, but it's all sorted now.

Saturday 17th December 2011
Crevasses and crampons
A very cold day today, -22°C windchill, so 2 x Lifas, windstopper, goggles on. Anyway, we left. Into crevasses we went. I led into some small hairline crevasses, then all of a sudden, large 'man-eating' ones arrived through which I had to weave the team – very difficult. But you get pushed left and right and can only go one way – out!

The crampon saga continues, and my feet seriously hurt at the end of the day. They are torture devices, but work! So I'm constantly tightening them and can't wait to get them off at the end of the day!

On Christmas Day I opened a present that my wife had packed for me: two pairs of fresh pants, and the other guys looked at them enviously. Never before has clean underwear meant so much! To have fresh, clean underwear, if only for one day, raises your morale. To be just a little clean down there helps enormously, psychologically!

Thursday 22nd December 2011
Antarctic Christmas
Awoke cold and to a total white-out/blizzard. Great! But Old Man Beardmore will not get the better of us today. We have decided to make today Christmas and we shall march

on Christmas Day. So all the trimmings came out, we made our Xmas phone calls, drank a hot chocolate with rum, Kev's punch electrolyte and gin and we have got Mark's half-a-bottle of Java whisky! Further to that we have got our penguin hats on! I opened my Xmas present – 2 x fresh pants and a trivia game (thanks my love – just what I needed). I gave Kev and Mark a packet of my pork scratchings and I brought out some Huntley and Palmer's biscuits (as used in the original Scott expedition). Mark also cracked the last salami out – so party time! Old Man Beardmore can stick that in his pipe and smoke it!

Friday 23rd December 2011
Stuck in the valley of doom!
This is the worst predicament we have been in so far. It is also the coldest so far: -33°C. More cold to come on the plateau I feel, but hopefully in a better place! But we are thinking positive and are making further plans for later to get to the Pole.

As I sit here the wind and spindrift is seriously buffeting our tent – my feet are warming up though. Will Old Man Beardmore release us from his prison? The Beardmore is not a nice place and by no means a place fit for humans! Horrible!!

At about 2100hrs we thought we saw a break in the weather, and it was a gamble, so we thought we'd go for it! Unfortunately, after some serious hills and the visibility back down to zero, seeing no depth in front, we called it a day.

Bizarrely enough, this was similar to what Captain Scott had faced. He wrote in his diary:

I write this sitting in our tent waiting for the fog to clear – an exasperating position as we are in the worst crevassed region... Since writing the above I made a dash for it, got out of the valley, out of the fog and away from the crevasses....

Never before has clean underwear meant so much!

Saturday 24th December 2011
Precarious situation
So, once again we wait. We are not risking this, like last night. So we are ready to go when the weather window appears. Not good really. Old Man Beardmore must be very angry with us!

Extract from my wife's diary:

Sunday 25th December 2011
You are one crazy, determined man, my love! I hope that this trip has been worth it for you and you got it out of your system. New priorities coming up!

Returning to my diary:

Sunday 25th December 2011
Frustrations camp
It's now 1430hrs. Had a pipe, brew and nap, but it's still a 'white-out' and now it's snowing again! This is pretty numbing, especially on Xmas Day!
   Well, just to pick us up, we have come up with a Christmas 'ditty' song for our audio in which we sang over the phone – what a laugh: '7 days of Christmas on the Beardmore'!
   1 – right leg in crevasse
   2 – broken pulks
   3 – broken crampons
   4 – tent-bound days
   5 – c-o-l-d toes
   6 – no visibility
   7 – days on ½ rats
   But the blizzard still blows. We have been thinking ahead: at the Pole and things to look forward to – positive thinking – scoff next!

Extract from my wife's diary:

"Had a pipe, brew and nap"

<u>Wednesday 26th December 2011</u>
I'm glad you finally managed to escape the worst of Beardmore. It has been very frustrating for you and us. You sounded a lot more positive having been able to move on and hopefully having broken the back of the glacier now. It's bizarre to think that you are marching right now as I am writing this!

Off the glacier with three or four weeks left, we worked well as a team which provided us with built-in redundancy, flexibility, and a good routine. We all stayed together as a team. At the end of every day ML would say, "Come on, let's do another kilometre for the Queen." So "One for the Queen" became a slogan, adding an extra hour, and going that 'little bit further'. Towards the end of the expedition Kev had lost so much weight that he was flying along, and in fact by then we were

Beardmore Glacier

opposites – we were struggling, whereas he had a sense of being imprisoned in Antarctica and wanted to get home. Now that I have children I can relate to how he wanted to get the expedition done and get off the ice.

The pressures were immense, with expectations from our sponsors, the association with royalty, doing this for Prince William and so 'for Queen and Country'. If we were to fail, we would let everyone down, including our regiment. We also had a certain amount of press attention, even though when we reached our destination, there were a load of guys playing cricket at the South Pole who took the spotlight! Unbelievable, but we were not there for the glory in the first place, so it did not matter, although it was quite sad and put our appreciation of modern-day polar exploration into perspective.

Approaching the Pole

All of us became very emotional as we approached the South Pole. The temperatures plummeted even further, but we were prepared for that, and I was glad that for the last few weeks I could actually wear the coat I had spent a fortune on.

The cold can be extremely aggressive, and once it gets into you, you just cannot seem to get it out, so you have to protect yourself in every corner. If there's a hole anywhere, the cold will find it, and then it will punish you. I still carry a scar on my face to this day where I was burnt by the searing cold. Of course, it's not clever to come back from an expedition with fingers missing. People might like to think that it's a war wound but, in actual fact, it's just bad administration.

30th December 2011
Extremely cold day
Everyone suffered with their goggles (even spares), they just seem to freeze up! Also, our balaclavas froze externally and internally which, attached to your beard, is not nice – extremely painful removing. I've just got patches where I ripped it off!
My right fingers are slightly white on the tips – a warning for me, I really must be careful! My jacket worked well, but could be longer and it's pretty hot!

The Race is More Nobly Won
Unbeknown to us, Team A made it to the Pole in 67 days. My wife wrote about it in her diary, but of course I couldn't write about it in mine, as we didn't know at that time:

Tuesday 10th January 2012
The Amundsen team arrived at the Pole yesterday morning. Although history repeated itself, I don't feel that you have lost. You had (and still have) a much more dangerous, longer route and you also had a lot more bad weather compared to Team Amundsen. I'm so proud of you and what you have achieved.
I feel a bit like I'm doing my own trek to the South Pole.

On our 76th day we had a gut feeling that they might be there, based on our delays, but we didn't know for sure. Eventually, we arrived at the South Pole with 25 minutes to spare, arriving on the same day as Captain Scott had done 100 years previously. That was quite something. In fact, we never planned it but that last day we walked for 20 hours just to get there on that date, with just those 25 mins to spare! Not surprisingly, the 17th January still has a lot of significance for us.

Sunday 15th January 2012
89° – the last degree!
A very long day today (13 hrs 50 mins on our feet – 12 hrs marching). We initially set off to a gloomy start: overcast with poor visibility. It was very flat for the majority with some hard pulling in fresh 'gluey' snow. But, so far, so good. Towards the end we hit a very large sastrugi field, which petered out to a flat 'salt plain' or even a beach! This is where we are now, pitched, only 41 miles from the Pole.

Monday 16th January 2012
Penultimate day.
Awoke very weary, but to bright and sunny weather! So spirits were high and positive to get going. It was a bit like Xmas Eve. So we set off aiming for 20NM. Initially I felt okay, but after 13hrs on my feet I felt fatigued! We hit some bad ground as well, high sastrugi and sandy snow. This definitely slowed us down. After all that we got 19.7MN which was not bad, considering. So, this leaves 22NM to the Pole – still achievable.

It was an amazing and emotional feeling getting to the Pole and achieving our goal. However, I would say that the previous week was the most powerful psychologically, as we approached the Pole and it became real. A mixture of huge feelings, then tears and thoughts of home, my wife and family, coming and going with every step I took forward. It was a very challenging journey, both physically and emotionally.

Thursday 17th January
Pole Day – 90°
So we've got 22NM to go to the Pole – let's hope the weather and ourselves can get through this. Writing this prior to leaving. Good luck!

'Always a little further'

Set off on our bearing for 5hrs, no sign of the station but we saw the planes coming in and then, hey presto, there it was, some 13NM away – the Pole! This provided us with a positive buzz, you cannot believe!! However, we lost it again, it went into a dip up until 4NM and then it was 2100hrs! Only 3 hrs to get to the Pole! We got shifting to get there in time and we moved. We were all working on empty – no fluids etc – hard! But – we got to the Pole at 2335 hrs – 25 mins to spare! We did it! We have just done the last degree in 3 days – quite an achievement! What an achievement!

We were met by Henry, arrived on 9th, looking a bit worse for wear! Anyway, we took a quick photo to prove we made it in time.

Arriving at The Geographic South Pole on 17 January 2012, 100 years exactly to the day!

Henry Worsley was at the South Pole to meet us. He looked a bit worse for wear and obviously had battled through all sorts to get there. We had a great time celebrating, and we also remembered those from Captain Scott's team who had fallen 100 years earlier. We crossed our skis and had a remembrance evening, each taking a slug of whisky from a small supply (thanks to a kind sponsor, although we had drunk the rest of the whisky supplies in the first two weeks!). The whole expedition had been a huge test for us mentally, physically, and also spiritually.

As a soldier, I might feel invincible in a 'bubble', but alone or in a small team of three, walking 76 days on ice, you feel very far from this. And this is not easy to admit, but I have to say that this was the hardest thing I had completed in my life, both physically and mentally, particularly compared to my military life, during which I have been exposed to all of the nice places of the world and looked the enemy in the eye!

It's worth mentioning that we made it into the history books. In order to be a recognised expedition and polar adventurer, you need to meet certain requirements, as Captain Scott and Roald Amundsen did. As we completed the expedition totally unsupported we entered the history books on a recognised website, Adventure Stats, and were ranked 9, 10 and me as number 11 to Captain Scott's expedition (see below). This is

AdventureStats.com
Keeping track of adventure history

Home
Adventure Rules
Statistics

Navigation

South Pole All Complete

		Name	First names	s	r	Nat	born	starting point	starting date	arrival date
1	1	AMUNDSEN	Roald			Nor	16.07.1872	Bay of Whales	1911/10/20	1911/12/14
2	2	BJAALAND	Olav			Nor	5/3/1873	Bay of Whales	1911/10/20	1911/12/14
3	3	WISTING	Oskar			Nor	6/06/1871	Bay of Whales	1911/10/20	1911/12/14
4	4	HASSEL	Sverre			Nor	1876	Bay of Whales	1911/10/20	1911/12/14
5	5	HANSSEN	Helmer			Nor	1870	Bay of Whales	1911/10/20	1911/12/14
6	6	SCOTT	Robert Falcon			UK	06.06.1868	Cape Evans	1911/11/01	1912/01/17
7	7	WILSON	Edward			UK	23/7/1872	Cape Evans	1911/11/01	1912/01/17
8	8	OATES	Lawrence			UK	17/3/1880	Cape Evans	1911/11/01	1912/01/17
9	9	BOWERS	Henry			UK	29/7/1883	Cape Evans	1911/11/01	1912/01/17
10	10	EVANS	Edgar			UK	2/3/1876	Cape Evans	1911/11/01	1912/01/17
35	35	WOODS	Gareth			Can		Cape Evans	1985/11/03	1986/01/11
36	36	MEAR	Roger			UK	2/15/1950	Cape Evans	1985/11/03	1986/01/11
37	37	SWAN	Robert			UK		Cape Evans	1985/11/03	1986/01/11
322		LANGRIDGE	Mark	2		UK		Cape Evans	2011/11/04	2012/01/17
323	289	JOHNSON	Kevin			UK		Cape Evans	2011/11/04	2012/01/17
324	290	VICARY	Paul			UK		Cape Evans	2011/11/04	2012/01/17

*Memorialising with a small service for those fallen
from Captain Scott's team during the expedition*

truly amazing and humbling, to have been some of the only people ever to travel in the footsteps of Captain Scott's ill-fated expedition on the same date 100 years later!

Diary 'On Reflection'

Initially, I knew this was going to be a tough deal but I didn't realise how hard. This was by far one of the hardest things I have ever done in my life! It has tested me both physically (strength and endurance), mentally (especially!), my emotional stability and spiritual well-being. However, I am proud to have followed in Captain Scott's footsteps and to have had the opportunity for a chance in a lifetime experience. I can see how Scott called Antarctica "such an awful place", but it has a beauty which he also noted. Antarctica controls you and not the other way around, and this is what we have found. I learnt a lot about myself, which

I will use from now on. We take our home comforts for granted. Facing this has made me really appreciate what we have – especially life!!

If you want a challenge and test, then there are still plenty of unchartered areas in the world to be visited; this is one of them. But, come prepared, read Scott's journal and be ready for a test of a lifetime.

Good luck.

Looking worse for wear on completion of the South Pole

Back Home and Heading North?

Having returned from the South Pole trip, and acquiring something of a taste for polar expeditions, it was during an evening fundraising event that we hatched our plans to head north. With the success of the trip south, and the knowledge and experience that we had gathered, it seemed obvious to attempt something else and try to raise money for a charity at the same time. Going north seemed like the obvious option.

As I cleared up from the event I discussed my idea of going to the North Pole with one of the team, Louis Rudd, and he was also interested. At that point we thought that we could do it as a pair and have it successfully completed within the year, although we both realised that we needed to get some background information and do some further preparation and training for the Arctic. We knew that the north would be a totally different landscape and environment to the south and would require different training and equipment. Where do you start?

Luckily for us, we had met a guy at the South Pole who had embarked on an attempt to walk to both Poles. Although his plans to cross the North Pole totally unsupported had not worked out for him, Mark Wood had actually been in this environment. He knew what kit to take, he had links with the logistics company, and was familiar with the route.

So we made some links and were invited to Mark's coming home and awards party where we first met him. He was obviously busy running the event that night, but I was particularly impressed by his education and community programmes. We managed to sit down and briefly discuss our idea with him, and he offered his support. In fact, Mark provided us with some 'food for thought' and also a bit of an ultimatum in that he wanted to be part of the expedition as well!

We discussed this on the way back in the car and decided to accept his proposal, partly because Mark had great knowledge of the Arctic, but I also liked the way Mark did so much for the local community with his schools and education programme. He had a good set of personal values and beliefs, something that I strongly believe in as well.

Mark would also be able to be the overt 'face' of the expedition, which was harder for us given our discreet backgrounds at the time. This could sometimes be very frustrating, not being able to say who we were or where we were from, whilst at the same time trying to make people understand that we were not amateurs. As a result, trying to get sponsorship and relevant logistical support proved difficult, as many people simply thought that we were 'ice virgins' and a lost cause, not worth investing in – after all, who were we? Just two soldiers after a free holiday or something?!

On a personal note, for every expedition there are also, of course, those loved ones that we leave behind. This has naturally been a feature of my military career, but to volunteer for a dangerous expedition is hard for even our nearest and dearest to comprehend. My late father used to say to me, "Why would you want to do something like this?" He could never understand my drive and determination to go and do things that were often dangerous and risky.

During the South Pole race my wife had experienced a particularly difficult three months because I had left her heavily pregnant. We both wrote diaries during that time, although her diary was somewhat different to mine when I read it upon my return, as has already been shown! To that end, I did not immediately reveal to her my plans for the North Pole, but unfortunately, she knew me too well and after six months she soon worked it out, so I broke the good news! However, having a very understanding wife, she knew she couldn't stop me. I must add that without her support, I would not have been able to do this. Partners play a very important role in our life journeys, and we should be very mindful and appreciative of their huge support and sacrifice. This is something which I very much realise now and, to be honest, I believe the medals I have gained for my service should have been jointly received!

By the way, the pregnancy resulted in the birth of Hugo Eric Scott Vicary, 'Eric' after my late father who sadly passed away shortly after the expedition (which was devastating for me and to be honest still hurts, as anyone who has lost a loved one will understand) – and, of course, 'Scott' after Captain Scott!

After our return, we had to attend quite a few events to celebrate and raise awareness and funds for our charities. One such event was a get-together for Prince William and Kate where, as our patron, he said a few words. Unfortunately, bringing my three-week-old son created quite a stir with the national press and hit the media and front pages, sadly, not because of the great expedition we had undertaken, but because the royal couple were looking at having their own children so stole the limelight! Some papers stated that my son had encouraged them to have a child of their own – some months later they did.

A nation turns broody

LITTLE Hugo Vicary is too young to know it but his meeting with the Duke and Duchess of Cambridge has set tongues wagging. Wills and Kate seemed very natural in his company. So fingers crossed that thanks to Hugo it will soon be all systems go.

Prince William meets my son and (inset) how the press reported the story

The Reason to Go

Nevertheless, the scene was set for the three 'musketeers' (or 'likely amigos') to venture to the North Pole, but to do what? In any expedition, it is important to have a valid reason to set off on what could be a high-risk trip. The mission needed to have good reasoning behind it and had to be based on solid values. This became even more important when talking to sponsors and securing the funding (for the South Pole we had this, in that we were raising funds for the Royal British Legion, as well as tracing the same footsteps as Scott and Amundsen in a centenary race).

During that first year, we soon realised that we needed to raise awareness for a good cause that matched our organisation's values. Firstly, to generate some interest, secondly to raise sponsorship, and thirdly to do something good! During the South Pole expedition, we had raised over £250,000 for the Royal British Legion (and it happened to be their 90-year anniversary at the time). The monies raised went to help build the Legion's new Battle Back Centres, where injured soldiers are given rehabilitation and can recover in brand new state-of-the-art facilities – something we were proud to have supported.

I would have hated doing anything as significant as walking to the North Pole for no reason at all. Unfortunately, some people do it just for themselves. For a start, even if we had only managed to raise a few thousand pounds for a worthy charity, it would have been beneficial for someone.

However, the issue of climate change soon became a very obvious topic to focus on. The importance of the mission was reflected in what was happening before our very eyes on planet Earth, highlighted, in particular, at the two extremes of our globe – the Poles! If climate change is happening there, then the knock-on effects for the rest of the planet must surely be significant?

Credit to Mark Wood, who came up with the concept of a 'Race Against Time' and undertaking the expedition to document what we saw on ice, to raise awareness for what would and should be called a crisis. Mark's education programmes, knowledge and experience of this field meant that having this as our expedition's core mission made a lot of sense.

At this stage, we were working with **Plan A**: to walk from the Canadian coastline, unsupported, pulling our own kit and supplies, all the way to the Geographic North Pole. Going from a coastline to a Pole is also recognised in the polar community. Back in 2014, it seemed like a great plan.

And so the preparation was underway....

Our goals can only be reached through a vehicle of a plan, in which we must fervently believe, and upon which we must vigorously act. There is no other route to success.

Pablo Picasso

4. The North Pole: Planning and Preparation

By failing to prepare you're preparing to fail.

Benjamin Franklin

Meeting Our Team

Teamwork was something that had become second nature to me during my Army service, in particular, working in small teams in often isolated and high-risk environments. Knowing and understanding who you're going to be cooped up with for weeks on end can be a help.

I already knew the previous team member, Louis Rudd, from the earlier South Pole expedition and, although he had been in a different team to me, I knew him through that training time. Louis was very driven and confident with his skills. Mark Wood was an unknown entity to be honest. However, for our training we ended up on two mini-expeditions to Norway where we got to know each other and built a great friendly rapport, especially sharing a similar sense of humour.

Unfortunately, due to the various setbacks, frustrations and lowering of our morale, Louis sadly pulled out of the expedition to focus on attempting his own expedition, which left just MW and myself. This was a shock for both of us, but understandable, particularly as we were not really getting anywhere at the time. Having learnt from my lessons in the South Pole, I felt that the benefits of working as a threesome outweighed those of going as a pair. You might have less room in your tent (and, believe me, space is something which you would very much yearn for), but a trio provides flexibility, built-in redundancy, and time to think. For example, when not leading you have longer to 'switch off' whilst you ski behind the other two. As for redundancy, in the worst-case scenario when something might go wrong, you may still be able to continue your mission as a pair. So the lack of a third person played on my mind, and when I mentioned this to Mark Wood he agreed that we needed someone else to join the team.

It was 17th January 2015, an important date for us and the polar world: Captain Scott's Day, the day that Captain Scott made it to the South Pole! The day on which he made it to the South Pole only to find himself beaten by the Norwegians. A date not so much to celebrate but to memorialise and remember. This was also the day when we had made it as a team 100 years later, in 2012, to the South Pole (with only 25 minutes to spare), and so a date that we often try to commemorate. It just so happened that on this date I was running an evening soiree at my place to celebrate this and had invited the guys who had been part of that team. We had a special South Pole cake, read some diary extracts, played some South Pole games (South Pole Family Fortunes) and ate some South Pole-related food (seal stew and the like – only by name, of course, in reality a fishy curry) and, of course, had plenty to drink! Some guests even came dressed up in ski gear, so it was a great evening!

Pipe-smoking had become an expedition tradition, enjoyed at home on special occasions

As we stood outside following the tradition of smoking our pipes, having a drink of Chilean red wine and reflecting on our times on ice, I asked whether there were any volunteers who wanted to come along with us to the North Pole. One member humbly declined with reasons which were valid and respected, but Mark Langridge said that he was interested. ML is a stalwart on ice and someone you would unreservedly follow into battle. He had previously walked solo to the South Pole, and again shared a tent with me on the anniversary expedition, so it would be great to have him onboard.

The following day I mentioned this to MW. He was slightly (and rightly) hesitant, because he didn't really know ML. I think I managed to alleviate his fears after explaining ML's fine credentials and so phoned ML, just to make sure that it hadn't been the wine talking when he had said "yes" the previous evening. Thankfully, he said he would still like to be part of the team.

So we were back to three and we gradually got to know each other. The importance of a team is being aware not only of your own strengths and weaknesses, but also of the strengths and weaknesses of the rest of the team. Then you can be aware and provide the right person for the right job, and also know when they may require some support. We each had our roles and special responsibilities, as well as our general polar skills (such as being able to set up the cooker, tent and look after ourselves). My specific role was as the medic, a role with which I was familiar after extensive training and having been a paramedic myself.

Our knowledge of each other and experience together increased through various meetings, including visiting sponsors, preparatory training and other organisation events. It is important to get to know each other quickly, both professionally and socially which, of course, involves a certain amount of humour and often happens over a glass of wine or three!

Charities and Sponsors
As I mentioned previously, I do not like doing expeditions just for the fun of it, particularly extreme ventures which may receive substantial attention. Having raised money for charities previously with the South Pole expedition for the Royal British Legion, cycled from Land's End to John O'Groats and London to Paris for a charity called Action Medical Research, which funds medical breakthroughs to help save and change

the lives of babies and children, the North Pole expedition also needed a charitable focus for whom we could raise money.

This became more apparent when, over a year into the expedition, we were not getting anywhere. When I was in Norway training with Mark Wood, we discussed the focus and options. In the end we decided to support a less well-known charity which was, nevertheless, doing good work, in order to give it the recognition it deserved, and which had particular links with the Armed Forces community, tying in with our own backgrounds. So, we did some research and decided on a charity called Hire a Hero.

Hire a Hero is a small charity based in Wales, led by someone from the same ilk and community, doing good work by putting soldiers into employment, particularly those soldiers who have difficulty transitioning from service into the civilian workplace. Research states that 5–10% of the Armed Forces community struggles to transition out of the military, a problem which can lead to mental health issues, homelessness or even suicide. It seemed like a great cause to us and so we met Gerry Hill MBE, founder of Hire a Hero, and explained that we wanted to support the charity, which he humbly accepted.

We also had some links with other organisations who would be able to sponsor us – relationships that would be mutually beneficial for all involved, including the charity. One example was Farm Foods. They supported our expedition and we linked them up with Hire a Hero. As a result, they managed to put people into employment and this relationship continues to this day. Hire a Hero recognises and recruits suitably identified service leavers and links them in with Farm Foods and their managerial programme.

We know from experience that those from the military have amazing skills and attributes which can be transferable when they leave. They just need a chance and an opportunity to demonstrate this – opportunities not easily found.

We had a great variety of kit and equipment sponsors. We trialled a watch by SUUNTO and did some product placement for them. Having learnt from the South Pole expedition about suitable food, which had to be high in fat, salty and light, Mr Porky pork scratchings were ideal. Chase Distillery, a small but impressive bespoke distillery selling a variety of quality craft vodkas and gins helped us organise some great events to raise awareness. We even had a small compilation of three vodkas named after each member of the team, in which I was marmalade vodka. I'm not sure why, as I'm not a red head! However, when we later gave some of this vodka to the Russians to try and help us build rapport, they complained that the drink was too sweet! I suppose they're used to something a bit cruder.

Change of Plan: Plan A Becomes Plan B

With three of us on the team, we had to make some serious decisions about our routes. Although Plan A had been to travel from the Canadian coastline to the GNP, the melting ice and the climate change that we were tasked to investigate meant that we had to rethink. After the 2014 season, we found out that Kenn Borek Air was no longer willing to take explorers out to the Canadian coastline to drop off at the start point due to the high risks, both physically and financially.

As in the South Pole, Kenn Borek Air was the expert aviation logistics company in the North to help get us to our start lines. They were our air taxi service – and believe me, they know what they're doing and can fly planes in the most extreme environments. Sadly, Plan A was now off the table and a 'no-go', so we had to go back to the drawing board and replan. This was bad news and a setback.

I remember the three of us in a hotel in early 2015, all stood around a map, trying to come up with a plan. Mark Langridge had some creative and 'out of the box' thinking about which way to go, and sometimes coming from our military world what people would see as crazy ideas do in fact work – the adage, 'who dares wins' comes to mind! However, the only other proven route to the North Pole was via Russia and so this became **Plan B**, from Cape Artichesky on the Russian coastline to the Pole. It had been accomplished previously, and seemed like a proven route and a sensible second option. And so the planning for this route began.

The Recipe for Success – PESTO

It is important that whatever task, mission or goal you want to achieve, you do the preparation, you put in time and effort, or even better, you have some 'P.E.S.T.O.' (Perseverance, Effort, get some Support, make Time and seek Opportunities).

A Bit of 'PESTO', the Recipe for Success!

Perseverance – and determination to achieve what you have been set out to do. It may be a programme, a project, a mission or an expedition, but you have to keep plugging away and not be put off by any obstacles in your way (easier said than done).

Effort – you have to put in the effort and the hard work required – you can't avoid it. An example was when I was preparing for the Antarctic, I would come home after a hard day's work and say hello to my wife, only to walk into the garage and then go on the treadmill or ski machine for a few hours. You have to make that effort, that preparation, not only physically, but mentally as well.

Support – having the support around you to be able to deliver what you want to achieve is important. That includes the friends and family who support you, but also sponsors, your place of work, etc. This may require that you give something back as a mark of mutual respect, allowing you to achieve what you aimed for. Support also includes professional support, advice, guidance, mentors, coaching, and the support of your team.

Time – make time. People are always saying that we are too busy, but it is how you prioritise and make time that matters. In my example of preparing for the Antarctic, coming home to do exercise in the evening, studying for my degree at night or during holidays – these were all ways in which I had to carve out and prioritise the time I had available to me, whilst also juggling my busy family life. Time should not be an excuse, it's all about how you manage it.

Opportunity – finding or making the opportunity. Sometimes the opportunity will not come to you, and instead you have to make it for yourself. That's exactly what happened, creating the North Pole expedition off the back of the South Pole, and the opportunity of the expedition grew from nothing. On the other hand, someone may give you a hidden opportunity which you may not value and you don't want to pursue, but you might be amazed that, by engaging with it, you could create possibilities and open some great doors for the future. In the course of a military career you might be sent on dreadful or pointless courses, but the openings they offer up may be surprising – meeting someone new, something happening whereby you can then harness those prospects, reframing them into positive and creative opportunities. This might mean saying 'yes' more often than 'no' and giving ideas a try.

Extreme conditions, particularly severe cold such as in the Antarctic or Arctic, present an environment that is unforgiving. Any mistakes can cause catastrophic injuries, force the mission to be aborted, or even worse, lead to death. The Arctic Ocean is an environment which tests just that, so your preparation needs to be on the ball! It's *bad* out there and I've had numerous instances where I have been caught out. The extreme cold can freeze bare skin within minutes and it can even freeze your pee… and I'm not taking the piss!

I remember my first wake-up call on this subject was when I first went for a 'number two' in Antarctica. I had my rationed tissues (one small pack for two days) in the side pocket of my jacket with the wrapper off, all good to go. I prepared myself, trying to find some cover, digging a hole and facing away from the wind. I 'snapped one off', removed my glove (placing my glove in my jacket) and opened up my pocket, only to have all of the tissues blown away by the wind! I learnt quickly how to have a snow bidet and look after my rationed tissues, and luckily I didn't freeze my arse again. I learnt from that experience!

Another example is setting up and taking down the tent. Of course, you're outside so you have all of your kit on, including thin gloves that you wear for dexterity and mittens providing warmth. As you work as a team collapsing the tent, you cannot take out tent pegs and do certain jobs such as pack your kit away without removing your large mittens. However, if you take them off for too long, you will soon become exposed to the cold. The danger is that you might not discover the impact of this exposure until a bit later.

This happened to me on one occasion. As we got moving and the blood pumped to my now freezing hands, they started to warm up. Anyone who has had this feeling of their hands warming up quickly after having been cold may be aware of the agony and intense pain it can cause to your extremities, particularly your fingers and thumbs, as the warmth melts the ice particles in your fingertips. The warm blood pumping to the tips of your fingers and reaching your nerves can be excruciatingly painful. On this one occasion it reduced me to tears, crying and shouting out as I marched at the front of the team. The rest of

Training in the lake at lake at the Warwickshire Hotel and Spa golf resort

the team never heard me thank God, as it was such bad weather, but believe me it bloody well hurt! This was a warning shot from the extreme environment, which does not take any prisoners.

The Arctic is a significantly different 'kettle of penguins' (excuse the pun!) to the Antarctic. Firstly, the wildlife is different, being home to polar bears and not penguins; the time difference from the UK is only one hour in the North, whereas in the South it's five hours; in the South the average temperature is -40°, whereas in the North it is -20°; and then of course there's the ice rubble and complete mess in the North. The Arctic is an ocean, and the ice is only a few metres thick. In some cases it's just sea, particularly due to the impact of climate change warming up and melting the ice. As a result, your pulk must be able to float, as must you, although without getting your kit wet. You therefore need a special pulk, as well as an easy to put on dry bag which you can wear over all your kit. This was all new information for us. Initially, we had to simply find out where we could buy this specialist kit, before we could even learn how to use it proficiently.

There are, of course, many transferrable skills. Any project or event might require specialist equipment, but the important thing is knowing how to use it, rather than simply putting it on and throwing yourself into the sea! The learning process needs to be conducted in a safe and progressive, stage-by-stage manner.

So, to familiarise ourselves with this new kit we chose a local swimming pool and practised, practised, practised until we found the best methods for getting in and out of our pulks, and using our foldable spades as oars to propel ourselves. Of course, in the beginning this was all in a nice warm swimming pool environment, before we then moved on to a lake at the Warwickshire Hotel and Spa golf resort. Here, we were joined by the local press watching us in action, so there was no pressure and, obviously, it was much colder than the pool! A good job we had prepared and, luckily, we had no problems.

Training with the equipment is one thing, but it is also important to train in an environment similar to the one you will actually be working in. For example, in a sport such as fell running, at some point you obviously need to get out on the mountains and start running. So as part of our training, we travelled out to Norway again. Unfortunately, ML could not join us on this occasion due to work commitments, so for this trip it was just me and MW. Unbeknown to me, this mini-expedition would also test my medical skills!

Pre-Training: Norway

Our trip to Norway was planned to be a seven- to ten-day expedition at a large frozen lake that I had previously used during the South Pole training. We hired an estate car which was just large enough for our pulks and kit, overnighting in Oslo. Having been to the location before and conducted a map recce of the area, we prepared our kit and drove out with our supplies to a lay-by. Stepping out of the comfort of our nice warm car we felt the sudden impact of the below-zero Norwegian temperatures. When we used this lake for our South Pole training, there was a layer of snow on it, giving our skis traction with our 'skins' stuck under the skis. However, now we had returned for the North Pole training, there was no layer of snow for the skis to grip onto with our special skins, and so the iced lake was too slippery for us to make any headway. If we had been using crampons, then fine, but not with skis, so we had to skirt around it on what snow was available on the edges, hoping to reach the northern edge within three days and then head back.

Before even getting into the car to set off for the lake, MW had been complaining about a bad back and had struggled to get about that morning. Nevertheless, we made some progress on what proved to be an ideal training ground, with the added benefit of being extremely picturesque. Having spent many years in the military, speeding about and not really soaking up the scenery, I now make sure that I take the time to appreciate my surroundings whenever I can. We only live once so it's worth doing, particularly when the locality was so beautiful. Sometimes the greatest expeditions are the ones you find and create yourself, giving an enormous sense of adventure, not knowing what is just around the corner. However, Roald Amundsen once said that, "Adventure is just bad planning," a statement with which I have some empathy.

Anyway, after about six hours skiing and crossing some dodgy ice, we pulled up and set up camp on a beach-like area. We got into our routine, had 'scoff', and then stepped outside to enjoy the clear starry sky and soak up the atmosphere. I lit my pipe, as I often do on these occasions, and reflected on the past and present, and looked towards the future. It all seemed pretty good at this stage.

The following morning, as we were getting up, MW suddenly let out a loud scream! He could not move – his back had gone into spasm and he was completely unable to get up. He was in excruciating pain. Anyone who has had a sudden onset of back pain knows how debilitating this can be, particularly as you're constantly sleeping on the hard ground whilst on expeditions. I have also been on the receiving end of this type of pain and have been off the road for a few days, but luckily I was at home at the time. It's not fun, especially when you're in an area of remoteness!

Anyway, I immediately went into 'paramedic mode', assessed the situation and instructed him to take some immediate pain relief, including paracetamol and strong anti-inflammatories. I devised a suitable and effective pain relief therapy, with what medications we had, that would work together over a prolonged period. I knew his pain was serious and that we could be there for some time. The car was one day's ski away, and we were some distance from civilisation. I left MW for a few hours to undertake a recce, as well as to think about what might be the best plan.

We had one casualty, with kit and equipment, and we were in the middle of nowhere. What could I do? In the military we have what are called Courses of Action (CoAs), the options open to you to achieve the mission. Well, our mission had changed and we had to abort and CASEVAC Mark. We had no choice. After conducting a suitable map recce, my plan was to leave Mark and ski back to the car which I could then drive back as close to Mark as possible. I had noticed a track about 3km away, so I could then load Mark into a pulk and ski-haul him to the car with our kit (or, if necessary, relay the kit). I discussed the plan with Mark and we both agreed on this CoA.

I set off with minimum supplies back to the car. Such a plan of travelling alone with very little is not advisable and should only be done in an emergency, because if something happens – falling through the ice, for example – then the risk of injury or death is high. I would only ever think of going on my own in such an emergency. Thankfully, I was fit and made great speed, but as I approached the car after several hours of skiing, I saw a large animal close to the car – a brown bear! Luckily, it must have been about 500m away and I don't think it saw me, but I did wonder how on earth I was going to get away from the animal if it started to approach me.

Luckily, as I paused, I saw the bear head towards the water's edge, where it probably found some food and then, luckily, it moved away. I cautiously skied to the car, catching sight of the animal's footprints and the hole in the ice where it must have caught a fish, and I made it to the car in a bit of a sweat! Once again, good training for the polar regions and the polar bears!

Safely in the vehicle, I headed towards the CASEVAC RV (rendezvous). I thought I could make it all the way on the track, but I fell short of Mark's tent by about 5km due to a barrier on the track, which was another obstacle and also frustrating, so I had to ski the rest of the distance. Remarkably, Mark had managed to get up, but he was still in a lot of pain, so he took the maximum pain relief possible before our intended move. Luckily for me he could walk/ski, albeit very, very slowly. I took all of the kit and after a few hours we made it safely back to the car.

Training in Norway

What a trek! A number of lessons were learnt on that mini-expedition, including the lesson that I had learnt many times before, that no plan survives contact! It was great experience for me with regard to emergency and rescue – something which you cannot prepare for. It was also valuable training for us with respect to what were to become many frustrated plans. I think Mark may have felt otherwise at the time!

Actually, on reflection, the setbacks and obstacles that you are confronted with should be seen as helping to grow and build your own and your team's resilience. In this way, exposure to pressures which may be out of your control can be seen as positive and valuable learning experiences. One thing is for certain – I've had a few!

Medical Preparation

As has been alluded to, it's worth mentioning briefly the importance of having medical support and protection during any expedition. It is critical, for without it the outcome could be disastrous and lead to potential death. Therefore, having suitably trained people with the right equipment is essential. This goes for any military operation, where trained medics and a support team would be present from the 'point of injury', right through the chain to the stage of handover to other professionals and, eventually, a primary healthcare facility (hospital).

Everyone in the team should have the confidence and ability to perform rudimentary first aid, which includes basic life support (giving cardiopulmonary resuscitation). Of course, the lead medic needs to be much more skilled than this, able to provide anything from minor to major medical care in those remote and extreme regions, where they may have to look after someone for a protracted period of time. Having the right training and equipment to perform the full range of medical procedures in these environments and look after your team, should an incident occur, is critical to the success of any expedition.

The problem facing the medic is that they are also a team member, having to look after their own health and do the job in hand, but also be responsible for the rest of the team's health as well as carrying the medical kit for 'every' eventuality. I remember one time, when I had just become a Troop Medic and I was on remote operations, my Troop Staff Sergeant came up to me and asked if I had some cold sore cream. At the time I did not, and therefore I was a 'shit medic' for not having any!

Needless to say, I took some the next time and learnt from this error. However, on reflection, should I have had it or should he have had his own?

Anyway, it is important as a medic or as any medical healthcare professional to be up to date, refreshed and to know what you're doing, understanding that you should work only within your trained parameters. However, when in a remote situation and knowing that there is literally no-one coming, where someone could die without an intervention, perhaps you would have to seriously reconsider this principle in remote and emergency situations. I was lucky in that I had been a trained Troop Medic, trained to the highest standards in advanced remote medicine, and I had become a State-Registered Paramedic on top of all of this training. I kept myself up to date and attended specialised training events. So, I was competent and had the confidence in knowing what to do.

As an example, at one extreme, I could perform dentistry – temporary fillings, something which I had done many times on operations to indigenous communities. Inability to sleep due to toothache is not good for performance so it's important to be able to help. At the other extreme, I could create a surgical airway if the basic airway manoeuvres would be unviable. In the case of a collapsed lung, I could decompress a chest and insert a chest drain if I had to. So, the expedition medic is a very handy person to have around!

When we talk about equipment, this is a difficult conundrum – not only carrying your own kit, but your medical kit to cater for every eventuality. A recommendation to get around this would be providing your team with a basic medical pack with all the items regularly used. For instance providing each team member with their own blister prevention pack, including Compeed and zinc oxide tape; providing Dioralyte should they lose valuable body salts due to a bout of diarrhoea; having their own lip salve and sunscreen as a heat preventative, etc. There is much more that could go into the individual medical packs.

The biggest drain on the medic during any extreme long-term expedition would be pain relief – something we learnt in the southern expedition, when I nearly ran dry! Therefore, taking plenty of pain relief and instructing the team members to take their own supply of paracetamol and ibuprofen is important. As the expedition medic I would just complement the personal medical packs with some extra kit, thus reducing my own weight

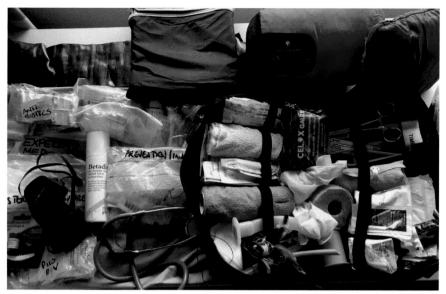

Just part of the comprehensive medical kit

in the process. I would also have my own personal generic medical pack and also the specific medication for my particular illness (at a weight of 6kg in my special box with my own injections!).

It is also worth understanding your own team's health and medication requirements so that nothing will be a surprise; it is always best to be forewarned and prepared. I would also recommend sessions with the team on medical training, to provide some confidence and basic skills. At the very least they should be up to date on basic first-aid – the ability to provide CPR would be reassuring for me!

As I've mentioned, the team medical pack would have to be as light as possible. I have mine down to 1lb and it should cater for minor and major medical events. (A list of items for both the individual and team medical pack is in the appendices.) I also complement all of my expedition medical packs with a stethoscope, a light-weight stretcher, cyalume lights, head torch, air marker panel and a SAM splint. If I was trekking somewhere without a tent, I would also take an eight-man bothy bag.

So, the medics' job can be a busy but important role, something which I have learnt on operations, training and on expeditions, and an incident often happens when you least expect it!

Funding the Mission

With any project, programme or expedition, you need the hard cash to be able to pay for the resources, the travel and the support in order to accomplish what you set out to do. This has always been true of expeditions, even from the very early days, with Roald Amundsen preaching to the Norwegian government and Captain Scott pitching to the 'dragons' of the Royal Geographical Society, with the aim of getting the financial backing and support they required. In fact, Scott was constantly worrying about money and trying to raise the required funds, even as he travelled south and stopped over in New Zealand. For expeditions of this nature you need a huge amount of funding. For the 'Race Against Time' we needed something in the region of £100k per person. How on earth do you get this sort of money and convince people to back and believe in you, especially if you're not on the 'famous' list?

Firstly, you need to find the right organisations and people. They need to believe in you and the reasons why you are doing this, and they need to see the trip as being mutually beneficial to them. You need to communicate, network, present and pitch to those potential 'dragons'. Understandably, many of these organisations often need to see some form of return. This could be anything from a product or logo placement, to more significant returns such as the adventurers providing leadership presentations upon their return. You often need to match their requirements and values with your own.

However, often the hardest piece of the puzzle is getting to the right person – the person in charge and, in particular, the person in charge of the purse strings! Cold calling rarely works; instead, networking is required to meet people who know people, who in turn know the right people that lead you to that sponsorship deal! This takes time, and is easier said than done.

During our first year, we thought we might be able to pick up where we left off from the South Pole trip. However, this had all gone 'cold' and we had no great leads to follow. We looked at every angle for support, making pitches for funding here and there, often at the wrong venue and often to the wrong people, resulting in no money in the bank. This was all very disappointing. These setbacks in themselves were debilitating, lowering morale and making our goal seem unreachable.

On one occasion we were invited to a rugby club where we were promised a significant group of potential investors. It was not until we got to this run-down old building and were directed to the rear of the venue to meet the contact, in what I would describe as someone's 'back room' complete with a makeshift bar, that we started to get a hint of what a waste of time this would prove to be. The man explained that people would arrive shortly. In fact, no-one turned up at all! That was the straw that broke the camel's back for us and, although it is always worth chasing potential leads, this experience made us sit down and rethink our strategy.

It was actually MW who got the first bite with a whopping £120K of support. I've always suspected that he sold his soul to the devil for that one! Nevertheless, what you often find is that when you secure one large investor who believes in you, others begin to follow. Potential backers start listening and realise that this planned expedition will actually become a reality, and so they start believing in you and your goals. This is exactly what happened to us. As well as financial help, we received other support in promoting the expedition with a range of sponsors. Each supporter and investor was incredibly helpful and by the back end of 2015 we had managed to secure all the sponsorship required and had the financial 'green light' to go ahead – a great feeling indeed!

Mental Preparation and Mental Fitness

I have learnt a lot of lessons in the military about having a healthy mind and being mentally fit. The importance of mental resilience should not be underestimated, affecting both physical as well as mental health (the two are always interlinked). Retrospectively, I also learnt a lot of lessons from the South Pole and its extreme environment, and that we're not invincible!

That said, mental strength is a hard concept to train for and measure. I think it comes down to what you have previously been exposed to, both physically and mentally, affecting your resilience and ability to 'bounce back' in any given situation. For certain types of training it is therefore important to try and simulate some of the pressures you may encounter, in a similar environment, if possible. I would say to the military guys I was training, that if you want to perform well on the hills, you have to get out and up on the hills in every type of weather. Likewise for a polar expedition, and hence why we spent time in Norway. Of course, you need to do other training too.

Anxiety

There will always be something outside of your control which creates anxiety, from aircraft crashes to an unseen virus which seems ready to pounce on us at any time. (The outbreak of Covid-19 has prompted an unprecedented and specific period of anxiety.)

If fears and anxiety are becoming overwhelming, it can be helpful to look at ways of coping to try and overcome them. A useful equation I use is:

$$\text{Anxiety} = \frac{\text{High estimation of danger}}{\text{Low estimation of being able to cope}}$$

So if you can increase your ability to cope, it is likely to reduce your estimation of danger and reduce your level of anxiety.

'Strong in mind, strong in body' is important, because if you are physically fit and able to conduct your mission or job (and so reduce the physical pressures), then this will enable you to focus mentally. Working on the physical side often exercises mental aspects as well, something which has been proven to help with overall well-being.

It can be good to allow some pressure during training through progressive and relevant exposure to stimuli, although being over stressed becomes unhealthy. Stress is an emergency response, which prepares the body for a given situation, whether fight, flight or freeze. The body is clever in preparing for this, with adaptations such as increased heart rate, breathing, adrenaline release, sweating, dry mouth, etc. However, if this happens over a prolonged period of time the stressors put on the body and your health build up and stress can be bad for you, potentially leading to mental illness.

I have learnt from my specialist military background that it is important to be able to know how you deal with stressful situations, particularly when your life depends on it. I was confronted eye-to-eye with the enemy on operations overseas and suddenly had a stoppage on the weapon I had. My training kicked in and I reacted automatically, something which had been drilled into me time and time again with this progressive training build-up, and something which I actually taught. It saved my life in this instance and believe me, that was a very close call!

It comes down to training, progressively building up in that environment where it becomes more and more difficult. For example, in the military, starting in a normal shooting range, and then moving into a dark, smoke-filled room in a building, full of friendlies and enemies. This is a much more difficult, high-pressured environment. Such exposure needs to be closely monitored, controlled and questioned. Obviously, training for a polar region is different, but similar incremental steps are necessary, from practising skiing technique in Germany to a mini-expedition in a cold environment such as Norway. You have to finally ask yourself, am I actually ready?

We needed strong mental preparation for the continuous obstacles we faced

How to approach and manage pain is also an important consideration. This would be especially relevant to us in the Arctic, where we would be pulling in excess of our own body weight across the ice and would have to endure both physical and mental pain. We know that usually, pain is only temporary but even so, we have to find ways of dealing with it. I am reminded by my wife of the pain experienced during childbirth – not that I know how it feels, of course, but I have now witnessed several births and the pain which my wife has gone through (three times in fact). It seems our brains are clever in not remembering the actual pain experienced at the time, thank God, as we seem to want to go through it again and again. This pain is similar to the Pole, although my wife and the rest of the child-bearing female population would definitely disagree! Coping strategies, such as distraction techniques, are very useful and powerful tools, particularly at the time of dealing with pain and stressors.

The body is a very advanced piece of machinery, even in dealing with pain, fear and suffering, and it is a piece of 'equipment' which we must look after, both mentally and physically. The more I understand this as a medic, with what I teach and do on expeditions, the more I realise how lucky we are and must look after our physical and psychological health.

Physical Training

Physical training is the tangible, measurable aspect of your health that you can work towards. However, physical training is not simply working up a sweat, but having the skills to be able to operate. For a polar expedition this would be to operate in extreme environments, the cold. Therefore, developing a progressive approach over time is important, and setting SMARTER goals is key to your success. You need a good run-up period to the main event to allow for a progressive step-by-step approach, and also time if things do not work out. A novice runner does not just turn up to a marathon and expect to get their best time, or even finish, if they have not trained progressively for some time. Additionally, the unexpected can always happen, such as getting an injury or developing a cold, and these risks have to be factored into the preparation as best as possible.

This can be broken down into a bit more detail with an example. For instance, a fit and healthy person wants to run a marathon.

> **SMARTER Goals**
>
> - **Specific**
> - **Measurable**
> - **Achievable**
> - **Realistic**
> - **Timely**
> - **Enthusiastic**
> - **Record**

Specific: To run in the London Marathon in 2022.

Measurable: I want to run it in under 3 hours 30 mins.

Achievable: I am fit, healthy, have no injuries and run regularly, so this should be achievable; if not then can you work on this area, but you need to ask yourself is it realistically achievable?

Realistic: I believe this to be realistic and not impossible based on the time I have to train and prepare, and what I have researched.

Timely: I have over a year to do this and will set myself weekly and monthly targets as well as run in at least two half marathons as part of my final preparation.

Enthusiastic: I really want to do this; it's part of my bucket list and I will also do it for charity.

Record: I will record and keep a diary of all of my training including nutrition, sleep, recovery, build-up training, times and setbacks, in order to see what works and what doesn't – learning from it and having a record.

I had been used to such training and preparation during my whole military career (although I had not formally realised or utilised the acronym). Preparing for the selection programme for my unit was very much the same and I applied this SMARTER principle throughout for my mini goals to help me reach my main goal.

In order to be able to pull a sledge and conduct your day's physical work over prolonged periods of time, you require a number of physical attributes – a mix of strength and endurance. When I say strength, it's not about being built like Arnold Schwarzenegger, but having strength across those key parts of the body, including the back, shoulders, legs and arms – those areas which will take a pounding, be jarred and jostled, as well as providing the all-important power. For example, when wearing your harness, your shoulders and back need to be capable of taking the huge strain. It is hard work! So during preparation you need to expose your body to these specific, physical pressures in order to improve performance – something which needs to be conducted progressively within a constructive programme so that you don't get injured and put yourself out of the game.

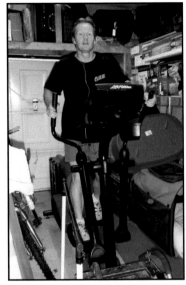

Training at home in my garage

It's a simple approach and a key lesson in life that can be applied to anything. Going walking in the hills but haven't even strolled to the shops for years? Start with a stroll, extend it to a few miles, add in some hills, and gradually build up with a programme. I hope you're getting my idea and message!

Physical training has moved on from spending hours in the gym with no plan or relevant programme. Today, it incorporates carefully worked-out strength and conditioning with lifting, building on strength, stability, core, conditioning and power. Polar explorers need to be robust and able to bounce back from the prolonged periods of physical exertion, as well as having the power to pull heavy loads. Such power comes from the legs, so for us training them was key, using beneficial leg strengthening exercises such as deadlifts and squats and, of course, time-building on your cardiovascular fitness, endurance and stamina, such as hill walking, is a must. Many polar explorers are often filmed training in the UK and elsewhere dragging tyres, which will undoubtedly have some benefits, although I think it just looks good for the camera! It's not something I have ever done myself – maybe I should?

As previously mentioned, I had been setting personal goals all of my life since childhood really, but was not fully aware of their importance and what I was actually doing. This is more formalised now, but came to the fore when I prepared for a rigorous selection process when I was 30 years old. I ended up with a huge folder of information, including what I did for the day, both physically and mentally, as well as what I ate and how I felt. This was a completely holistic approach. As an example, although I was not allowed to do the summer selection as I was due to go away on operations to Bosnia for six months with my unit, I used it as a positive to start preparing mentally and physically. I produced a programme to help me achieve my first mini goal, which was to run the April 2000 London Marathon in under three hours 30 minutes. I thought this was realistic and achievable, and it matched the SMARTER principles. I had a bit of work to do, as I had never run a marathon before! I had run half-marathons and was pretty fit, but I had to prepare for this. The aim was to use this mini goal to get me CV (cardiovascular) fit for the marathon. The next mini goal, would be to start wearing boots, kit and equipment and then increase the distance, the terrain, etc. That was the next phase.

However, when I was in Bosnia I went running nearly every day, increasing the distances and building on my endurance. I actually really enjoyed this, as it was something to look forward to at the end of the day, and running around Bosnia was so picturesque, seeing the culture, scenery and people. I would run for hours – it was my escape and time to think! I felt a bit like Forest Gump at times. Towards the end of my time there, the unit ran a small race which I entered. I pushed myself, did a good time and I realised that I was doing well, which gave me confidence that the actual London Marathon was achievable. In the meantime, I read running magazines to help me understand the best trainers, clothing, what to eat, pre-event training, which running group to be in, etc, all of which was very helpful. And don't forget that when recovering from physical activity, you can work on preparing yourself theoretically.

Immediately on leaving Bosnia I entered the London Marathon, joining the Runners World 3:15 hrs group. I realised that if I let things slip I would still be able to come in under 3:30 hrs. Anyway, I'm glad that I did, and guess what? I came in at 3:27 hrs, achieving my first mini goal! The next mini goal was a mountain marathon, which I completed successfully. All towards my ultimate goal – passing selection.

Nutrition and Hydration

Nutrition is simply having the right amount of healthy fuel (calories) to put into our bodies to generate the power needed to conduct any daily task efficiently. On an expedition, nutrition means something slightly different to the healthy balanced diet you would be having at home in a 'normal' life (even though it is always important to understand what you are putting into your body for optimum performance). When undertaking some form of endurance expedition, it comes down to calories and eating enough of them to achieve the right effective balance.

On a polar expedition you potentially burn between 5–6,000 calories a day (compared with 2–3,000 in a normal environment) and this needs to be constantly replaced. Food provides you with relevant and suitable energy, although in the Arctic it's not like being at home and trying to eat healthily! Instead, you need fats, carbohydrates and high-calorie foods. Our main sustenance was in the form of a range of 800-calorie expedition meals, prepared in a variety of menus, to which you simply melt ice and add hot water. We had to select which foods we would like

Sat on a pulk eating Mr Porky's

and order the meals we thought we would want in advance (see appendix). I tried eating some of them at work to see which ones I preferred. In a normal working environment one meal filled me up with enough calories for lunch and dinner (which my wife wasn't too pleased about!). Having a varied menu was important to prevent monotony, provide something to look forward to and, believe it or not, your taste buds change out on the ice. In the South Pole my favourite foods became the foods I disliked the most, so a variety of food was a good thing. On the expedition we also needed high calorie snacks to see us through the day, so we carried a 'nutty bag' which would include simple and complex carbohydrates such as flapjacks, chocolates, sweets and nuts. The fattiest nut is actually the macadamia, although also the most expensive!

One lesson learnt from the South was that our bodies craved certain foods – in particular, salt. We possibly lacked certain minerals and vitamins, although I was taking micro-nutrient supplements with my daily cod-liver oil and multivitamin supplements. Thinking this through,

Snacks laid out, ready to pack

it seemed that pork-scratchings would be an ideal expedition food. They are coated in salt, full of fat and are lightweight, as well as being pretty tasty. So having Mr Porky's Scratchings as a sponsor was ideal! Further to this, we had another sponsor provide us with beef jerky, also high in protein and salt – a key snack to look forward to during and after the journey, as well as providing vital protein required to aid recovery.

Taking in food and maintaining energy levels is key over a prolonged and exhausting day. Failure to stop regularly and refuel would result in loss of power, loss of concentration, tiredness and a drop in performance, which you cannot afford to happen. We would usually stop every 1–1½ hours to 'fuel up' for about ten minutes, before changing around and moving on, doing it all again numerous times during the day along the 'white treadmill'.

Alongside nutrition you need hydration – replacing fluids and body salts. In the UK under normal conditions, it is recommended that you should be looking at drinking approximately two litres of fluids per day. Obviously, in hotter climes this would be increased, depending on what activity you're doing. For us in the polar regions, two to three litres during the day sufficed, as we did not lose any through sweat and we didn't want to. This was achieved by drinking warm/tepid water from prefilled flasks. I would carry one flask with water and another filled with a different flavour electrolyte solution (which had been added to the flasks each morning). This took time to prepare, but it was vitally important. I would also take with me my small insulated Thermos mug carrying a second brew from the morning to last for the first hour. This was a nice luxury and very well received when I stopped on my first leg in the mornings and cracked open a hot chocolate.

However, on some days, particularly hotter days, we had to get some water melted and drunk immediately once the tent was up. In dire situations we added ice to our flask along the way, although this was very rare. We also drank hot beverages in the morning and evening. I would drink hot chocolate (high in calories) in the evening with my meal, as well as for breakfast. I never went for coffee, because it is a diuretic and will get you pissing constantly, something that is not helpful in Arctic conditions! I grew to love my hot chocolate out there, but would rarely touch it at home. The same was true of chocolate in general and I had a love–hate relationship with it on ice.

Food Data for North Pole Trip
Calories and weight (kg) for 65 days

2 x mains & 1 x pudding per day

　　　Wt: 410g Cals: 2100

Drinks: 3 x hot choc or isotonic for flasks

　　　1 x hot choc for evening
　　　1 x coffee for morning
　　　Wt: 240g Cals: 800

Snacks (combo of everything we have of my choice)

　　　Wt: 570g Cals: 2840
　　　(1.22kg total food wt)

Fuel: 10L = 6kg
　　　(+ containers + 4 full Sigg cooker botts to start)

Total food weight per day
(inc toilet roll, wet wipe, vitamins, etc.):
　　　1.4kg/ 3.08Lb

　　　65 days' food = 91kg/200.2Lb
　　　Total cals = 5740

Careful planning of your menu for the duration of an expedition is crucial. (See appendix for a chart of my fuel.) In the South Pole we only had enough rations for 70 days and we skied for a total of 76 days. As a result, we had to reduce our ration intake, preserve food and move to half-rations in order to finish. This was a very difficult but essential decision that was taken in order to achieve success. The danger of this decision was that it affected our energy levels and power, because we did not have enough calories to replace those we were expending

Mark Wood preparing his food

through skiing. Then again, if you do not have enough food, that means mission aborted and finished!

Preparation of food takes time. We would line up all our food and snacks and package it up for each day as our daily ration. For the week, this also included a toilet roll pack, wet wipes, tobacco for the pipe and some chewing gum (one piece for each day). It would then all be sealed in a waterproof bag for the day to prevent any contamination should the fuel leak (something which has been known to cause mission failure for some expeditions). All of this is then placed in a waterproof bag for the week and marked up 'Week 1, 2, 3, 4,' etc. Finally, it is all weighed to ensure you are pulling the correct weight.

Obviously, on any self-sufficient, unsupported expedition, weight is a crucial factor and trimming it down within sensible reason is very important. Mark Wood removed all the food packaging, added his own spices and then made the bags much smaller. I preferred my option of eating the food in the original packaging and then using those bags to hold rubbish and prevent any cross-contamination or food poisoning. It was an individual decision, and each method had its pros and cons.

Whichever we chose, this level of detailed preparation all takes time but is key for an expedition of this nature. Failing to prepare is preparing to fail!

Sad News

I was in Germany with the Army, taking some students downhill skiing, as well as training for the North Pole expedition. At the same time, Henry Worsley was attempting to complete the first solo and unaided crossing of the Antarctic, in the footsteps of his polar hero, Sir Ernest Shackleton. From what I had seen on the social media that I was tracking in the latter stages of Henry's expedition, I thought that he really didn't look well. Then, one night, I received a phone call from Louis and the devastating news that Henry had sadly passed away.

Training in Germany

He had crossed more than 900 miles, but exhaustion and bad health had forced him to call for help 126 miles from his journey's intended end. He was rescued and flown to a hospital in Punta Arenas, in southern Chile, where he was diagnosed with peritonitis. Sadly, he later died in hospital, aged 55.

The news was extremely upsetting, not only for me, personally, but also for the team. Henry was not only our friend and our patron for the 'Race Against Time', but it had a ripple-effect across everyone in the polar and exploring communities. I continued to train in Germany for our expedition, often with a tear in my eye. It had a huge effect on me.

However, the show had to go on and as we prepared for our mission, Henry's death was often on my and, no doubt, the team's minds. Nevertheless, it also gave us inspiration and strength – we will do this, we will deliver this, for Henry. He was to be very much in our hearts and minds as we were plugging along, feeling that he was with us. He'd never been to the North Pole, so it was good to have him with us in spirit, although I'm not sure what he would have thought of the environment!

We all attended Henry's funeral in London when we came back, which, obviously, was a very emotional event. We met old and new friends who knew Henry and had taken part in his previous expeditions. We all had our own reflections about such an inspirational polar legend. We took solace in the fact that he had been doing something he loved and that meant so much to him. A bitter-sweet pill to swallow for all who had loved and admired him.

The entry for Henry in the Encyclopaedia Britannica reads as follows:

Henry Worsley, (Alastair Edward Henry Worsley), British soldier and polar explorer (born Oct. 4, 1960, London, Eng.—died Jan. 24, 2016, Punta Arenas, Chile), unsuccessfully attempted the first entirely unaided solo trek across Antarctica in an effort to complete the 1914–16 cross-Antarctic expedition planned by Sir Ernest Henry Shackleton, whose party was shipwrecked in the heavily iced Weddell Sea and had to be rescued. (Worsley's expedition was also intended to raise money for the Endeavour Fund, a charity that provided aid for wounded service members.) Worsley departed on the 1,770-km (1,100-mi) trek from Antarctica's

Ronne Ice Shelf on Nov. 14, 2015, and reached the South Pole on Jan. 2, 2016. He was only 50km (30mi) short of his intended final destination on the Ross Ice Shelf when exhaustion and illness, combined with blizzard conditions, compelled him to call for help on January 22. He was airlifted to a hospital in Punta Arenas, where he succumbed to bacterial peritonitis. Worsley had headed two previous expeditions

Henry Worsley

to Antarctica. In 2008–09 he led a party along the route that Shackleton had used in 1907–09; Worsley, however, reached the South Pole, whereas Shackleton's team had been forced to halt 180km (97 nautical miles, or 112 statute miles) short of the pole. Worsley returned to the continent in 2011 in commemoration of Norwegian Roald Amundsen's successful trek to the South Pole in 1911–12 as well as of the ill-fated 1910–12 expedition led by Amundsen's British rival, Robert Falcon Scott. Worsley retired in 2015 from the British Army as a lieutenant colonel after a distinguished 36-year career that included stints in Northern Ireland, Bosnia and Herzegovina, and Afghanistan. He was made MBE in 1993 in recognition of his service in Northern Ireland.

Plan B Becomes Plan C

The end of 2015 and the start of 2016 brought yet more setbacks, and more disappointments. The sad death of Henry was bad enough, but prominent in the international news at the time was the public inquiry into the killing of a former Russian spy, Alexander Litvinenko. Little did we know the effects this would actually have on our planned expedition. He had been poisoned in 2006 by a radioactive substance whilst living in the UK, and in January 2016 the inquiry concluded that his murder had no doubt been approved by Russian President Putin. Diplomatic relations between London and Moscow took yet another drastic drop, sadly affecting our expedition.

On the positive side, by early 2016 we had the money, and our expedition had the 'green light' to go. With such optimism about our mission to travel to the North Pole, I was in Germany skiing when I received the news that the Russians had refused our group transit visas, a crucial document to enable us to travel through Russia and arrive at the right departure point. Without permission to travel to and through Russia, our plan to go from the Russian coastline to the GNP was scuppered. There was no getting around the lack of visas.

So we had a period in 'no-man's land' when we didn't know what was happening, and we had no idea what to do. We decided to keep it to ourselves for a while, and not to inform our sponsors or supporters. We had the money now, but nowhere to go and no logistic support! I guess, in essence, we were also still in mourning for our friend Henry, and also for our seemingly now failed mission, just trying to come to terms with how to get through these setbacks. The situation was extremely difficult on us as a team, creating frustrations and emotions, all of which again seemed out of our control.

Bizarrely, it was at Henry's funeral that, through Steve Jones from Antarctic Logistics Expeditions (ALE), who made a link with the Canadians. I knew Steve from our previous expedition to the South Pole. In fact, anyone who ventures that way will know Steve, as he is the Operations Manager for ALE who monitors, supports and advises expeditions. All in all, Steve is a very knowledgeable and connected guy with regards to the polar world and extremely friendly, helpful and just a good bloke!

At the funeral, Steve asked whether he could help us. Funnily enough – yes, he could! The old adage, 'You don't get if you don't ask' springs to mind here! So we asked if the Canadians would be able to provide some aviation support. However, on Plan A, they had publicly pulled out and were not supporting any expeditions, so this was a long shot, but we asked them if they would be able to lay something on for us, as a one-off. The Canadians had said they could, but insisted that we had to travel from the Pole to Canada and they would support us about half of the way and then pick us up. The Russians would cover us from the GNP until three degrees.

And so Plan C was born. Not the Canadian coastline to GNP (Plan A). Not the Russian coastline to GNP (Plan B). But GNP to Canadian coastline (Plan C). The plan would be that the first three degrees would be operated under Russian support, but as soon as we had walked those three degrees we would cross over into Canadian territory and head south to the Canadian coastline, supported by the Canadians. Sounds like a plan!

It's bizarre how, by this stage, our initial plan had already changed twice. Once again, no plan survives contact.

We've all had to adapt to cope with a pandemic. Climate change will force far harsher changes on our kids. All of us should follow the young people who've led the efforts to protect our planet for generations, and demand more of our leaders at every level.

Barack Obama, Earth Day 2020

5. Ready to Go?

23rd March 2016
After 3 years in the making with setbacks and obstacles in our way, it looks like a goer. This is 5 years from when I last set off down South in what would be one of the hardest things I have ever done in my life – and now I set off again, to what I believe will be even harder – why? Good question.

Spitsbergen

Loaded up with all my equipment (and there was a lot of it!), I travelled by van to Heathrow airport where I met up with the others. The van was packed with 28 boxes of kit, which included our rations, tent, skis, other equipment and pulks. It proved an epic challenge for baggage handling, as we each had four trolley-loads of equipment, and pushing this around an airport was our first test of endurance and logistics! Luckily, we grabbed an airport representative from the airline who helped our check-in run smoothly. In addition to this huge amount of baggage, we were also carrying a rifle complete with ammunition for protection against polar bears (not on the flight, of course), which had to go through the correct luggage channels. (Don't worry, we didn't have the gun on the actual flight with us.) ML had to prepare the appropriate paperwork to prove ownership and get the gun through various checks and, thankfully, this went through amazingly smoothly without any problems.

We flew to our first stop in Oslo, where we were told that all our kit would be loaded onto the next aircraft to Longyearbyen, on Spitsbergen Island in Svalbard. Landing quite late, we went to baggage reclaim to retrieve our overnight bags. In the midst of the usual chaos at baggage

The team with our kit, ready to go

At the airport, ready to go... with so much kit!

reclaim, as we saw our boxes and pulks circulating on the conveyor belt, we realised that we would have to offload it all. What we had been promised did not prove to be true (a lesson to be learnt there!) and it was just luck that we were there to claim our personal baggage for the night! We duly offloaded our kit and then pushed out a train of trolleys to an overnight storage, for which we had to pay extra. Exhausted, we then left for a local airport hotel to rest our weary heads, ready for an early start. Important lesson: you should always factor in extra costs and problems within any expedition. Unbeknown to us, this was just the start!

The following day we were up early, refreshed and ready for the next leg of the journey, going through the same rigmarole as we had at Heathrow. After four hours' flying, we landed in Longyearbyen, the closest town to the North Pole which would also be our base for the next week – or so we thought. Of course, back in the day our historic polar counterparts would have sailed by ship for weeks on treacherous seas just to get to their starting points, if they made it there at all! Thankfully, that was not something we had to endure.

Longyearbyen was absolutely freezing! We were picked up from the local airport by a large taxi-van, roomy enough for all our bags and kit, and made our way to our lodgings. These were in old coal mining cabins, accommodation blocks to the north of Spitsbergen, complete with a restaurant and bar, a small souvenir shop and a place to socialise and chill. The coal miners' cabins were ideal for what we needed, offering a basic room each where we could start preparing, and enough room so that the pulk and kit could be laid out. Thankfully, the cabins made day ski trips possible, literally from our doorstep out into the icy wilderness. We still had to be armed, and everyone leaving on skis had to carry a rifle in case of a polar bear encounter. It was quite bizarre to see people walking round carrying rifles!

Without knowing what was to come, we were glad to be in Spitsbergen, initially. This was essentially the starting point of the expedition, our 'patrol base', launch pad and training ground before the walk to the Pole. We were to be conducting our final preparations and

In the cabin with our kit

training here, aiming to fly out on 1st April – or was this just an April Fools' joke?!

> ### 24th March 2016
> *First impressions Svalbard is that it is right up my street – snow-covered mountains, very cold and has like-minded people. It is a bit like Chamonix but extreme. A great base to work from, for our final preparations.*

> ### 29th March 2016
> *The Russian, Leo, arrived at 2030hrs and he sat down to discuss and update us on things. It's all looking good for the 1st April!! This is it! We were told that the main man, Victor, from the Russians will be arriving tomorrow to discuss details. So far, so good!*

> ### 30th March 2016
> *We did not see Victor today as he had not flown in and we arranged to see him tomorrow – let's see what he says!*

The accommodation provided great food, but as everyone knows, it can be extremely expensive in Norway. Costs started to rise. At the beginning the miners' cabins were a novelty but, unfortunately, they soon became a depressive place and 'cabin fever' began to set in.

Cabin Fever

From the beginning the expedition had experienced some major frustrations – from not getting any sponsorship to the Russians refusing our visas at the last minute.

Once in Spitsbergen we had thought that we were literally ready to go, and anticipated leaving as planned. However, as the days passed, we kept receiving news of cracked ice runways, and our frustrations began to set in. As with any expedition, we were prepared to undertake a mammoth mission on a tight timeline, constrained by our logistics company and the environmental and seasonal changes including, of course, the rapidly changing ice and the ever-moving sea. All of these things were having a massive impact on the team and me, and we hadn't even left yet!

Constantly being given bad news via the Russian logistics company, basically that we could not start, had the knock-on effect of lowering morale, increasing frustrations with the company and their people, feeling vexations at the environment, and being irritated within ourselves.

31st March 2016
So, we had to go down to meet the legendary Victor for 12.30pm. We met him at our nice café and discussed the departure, logistics and other parts with him. A nice 'jolly' chap with a huge polar history and he seemed friendly enough (they often do...). He said that they had problems with the plane and that hopefully we should still be away tomorrow (night) or on the 2nd. If I'm a betting man, I bet it will be on the 2nd April – we'll see.

We had to vacate our rooms on several occasions because we had only booked them for a week, and more people were coming to the base. This forced us to move elsewhere, first to another floor, then another block. With all of our kit this was painful, expensive and created a cabin fever all of its own.

1st April 2016
We will check out and pay, then move into our new flat. This we did and it was a 'ball ache' to carry the very heavy pulks from the rooms. It also took an age. Viktor called saying that we should be taking a further five days rations. Nothing about the flights until he called again, saying that it now would be tomorrow. The first flight would be proving the runway in the morning and we would be next in the afternoon – apparently. We'll see, eh?

We tried to break up the frustrations with regular ski treks, practising our tent routine and sleeping out (which, of course, also reduced our overheads). Through this we tried to stay focused and maintain a routine, but it became difficult when days started to go by. We hadn't yet walked a single mile on the Arctic Ocean, where we should have been. We desperately needed to get on the ice to meet the timelines, or it would be failure before we had even started.

2nd April 2016

Had a late brekky and then we received the call from Viktor – bad news!! The runway has a crack in it and therefore will create more delays… Grreatt! So, we're kicking our heels yet again. To be honest this is not good, quite depressing and a lowering of morale, but I always think things happen for a reason!

NORTH POLE 2016: RUNAWAY RUNWAY

RUSSIAN GEOGRAPHICAL SOCIETY

A massive crack running along the first half of the 1,200-meter ice runway at Barneo gives an An-74 airplane very little room to land and stop Monday.

WASTED ON CRACK

North Pole hopefuls facing more than a week of delays as ice runway cracks before Barneo opens

By MARK SABBATINI
Editor

This year's North Pole expedition season may be the worst ever for modern adventurers hoping to reach the top of the world, as the opening of the Barneo ice camp will likely be delayed more than a week due to ongoing problems building a stable ice runway.

A runway at the support camp at about 89 degrees latitude north was completed Sunday – a day or two later than officials hoped to

See SHATTERED, page 6

3rd April 2016

Mark W has just arrived and told us that Viktor has been in touch and good news – the technical flight is leaving later and we should be away after that.

News just in – here we go – Viktor called again to say that we <u>won't</u> be flying tonight now! Apparently fly out tomorrow.

106

I read a good number of books to help pass the time and this has a calming effect. One particular book was *The Chimp Paradox* by Steve Peters, all about controlling your inner chimp and frustrations (which I felt was very apt!). When I finished reading it, I wrote a small paragraph in the front and signed it, leaving it for some other traveller. Oh, and did I forget to mention that I also completed a distance learning course? Some indication of the amount of time we had on our hands to occupy! However, it is worth noting that healthy distractions such as education, are key ways of coping during any crisis. This worked for me and kept me focused, and also distracted me, during frustrating times.

With all of this waiting around we were trying to remain sharp and focused, although on a few occasions we had a beer (or three) to drown our sorrows about facing yet more delays. As Mark L would say, a couple of quiet ones and ten loud ones! Unrestrained, this could have been an unhealthy diversion, although at the time it helped distract us from a dark period. We also reduced costs by eating some of our spare rations – extra fuel that we had brought along as contingency (although mainly intended for emergencies out on the ice).

I cannot fully explain how depressing and frustrating this period was, but believe me it was an incredibly difficult time. We were pulled from pillar to post changing our rooms, our routine was upset, the financial implications were serious, and we experienced time delays and misinformation. All of this got on top of us and most of it was out of our control, yet again. It negatively impacted our emotions. After all, we just wanted to get on with the mission in hand, to document what we saw on ice.

As both the climate and the Russians were out of our hands, it created a period of anxiety. Some of the classic yet subtle signs of anxiety started to reveal themselves, such as anger and worry, and looking for ways to cope with these emotions. Being unable to deal with things because they are beyond your control can create anxiety which, of course, we were not immune to. As a team it was a short step to start bickering between ourselves and some kind of 'blame game'.

4th/5th/6th April 2016
I write this sat in our tent – no, not at the North Pole unfortunately – still in Svalbard!! We have just got our pulks

back from those damn Ruskies and we have decided to go and do some training locally from the airport.

It really is bad news and a huge delay due to there being a crack in the ice at the runway in Barneo – they initially thought they could fix it, but after 24hrs of poor communication and bad news from the Ruskies they have got to find a new one!! It could take 5–7 days!! This, obviously, is a game-changer for us, due to the time involved, and we sat down at the hotel to discuss our options. We were all adamant we should continue as planned, as the whole aim of the exped is to document climate change. We also had to move out of our rooms again, only to move back in again – that's three room moves so far. It's been a logistical nightmare and it's not finished yet.

After the third week and numerous setbacks, we started to question everything. What had started as a novelty had turned into a nightmare. What could we do? What options did we have left if things were to fail? Had we failed? Have we done the right thing? Should we just cut our losses and go home? But then we would be letting our followers, our supporters and ourselves down. All sorts of uncertainties started to fester in our minds and blur our vision of the original mission.

What's the 'take home' message from something like this? Try to remain calm, obviously. And when you cannot influence something outside of your control, control your 'inner chimp' instead. Be mindful of how people can react differently to various situations, and be able to reassure, support and communicate with each other.

7th April 2016
We received some devastating news, that the second runway they were looking at has got a crack in it!! This is a further game changer. Morale in the camp was not good. My thoughts were racing to what is recoverable and credible – what can we do? Is this it? Devastating, but I was thinking positive and thought that rather than giving up (as the other guys were thinking) we should at least do something – even the last two degrees!!

Trying to look upbeat after receiving yet more bad news

The problem now is accommodation, as a massive backlog of people was mounting due to the Barneo problem. All we want to do is 'explore'! Is this the last time, or have we been beaten by climate change?

Many people who venture to the Poles claim they have been on massive expeditions there but, in fact, they have actually been guided most of the way and have only done the last degree, which is about a week's worth of expedition on ice. This is fine for some people, and I do not wish to belittle great achievements, but we wanted to make it a unsupported and unguided expedition on ice, hence the reason we were trying to push it as much as we possibly could. As a minimum we wanted to travel as far and for as long as possible, but it was up to the Russians and dependent on how long they were prepared to risk staying on ice, especially given the time that we had already lost.

Key for us was to try to recall the reason why we were there. What was our mission statement? What were we trying to achieve there? Our task was to document climate change, although we weren't just documenting, we were experiencing it first-hand, and being frustrated by it.

In any situation, if you go back to the mission statement, you'll take meaning and strength from that. Don't lose heart when everything else is failing around you. Stay strong and remain positive.

Mission reminder: To document what we saw on ice!

Plan C Becomes Plan D

Going from Plan C to D was our last-ditch attempt to retrieve something good from what was now a collapsing situation, and this was a difficult decision to make. As we were completing another night out training, we received the dreaded phone call from the Russians, with yet more bad news that proved to be a game-changer. The Russians had informed us that the runway had cracked yet again, creating more delays, making it now impossible to reach Canada safely in the time we had available. The ice would have broken up by this time, plus the logistics company were not prepared to take the risk. This was devastating news for us.

However, as we skied on, reflecting on this terrible news and thinking that we would be getting on the next flight back home, I had a 'lightbulb' moment and stopped in my tracks to explain to the team that we still had a number of COAs available. These were: (1) jump on a flight and call it a day; (2) fly out and return the following year (difficult due to work constraints and sponsors); or (3) speak with the Russians again and persuade them to change the plan to drop us off as far as they could, and we then walk from there to the Pole – at least we would still achieve our mission!

We unanoumously decided on giving COA 3 a punt, our only option to salvage and save this expedition. COA 3 would still be able to keep our mission statement alive, by documenting what we would see on the Arctic Ocean. So we raced back to explain our change of plan to the Russians. We tried our hardest to get dropped as far away from the North Pole as possible, but due to safety and time restraints, the Russians would only allow us to be dropped off at 88 degrees (the last two degrees, approx 150 miles), so we had no choice and agreed. This was now Plan D!

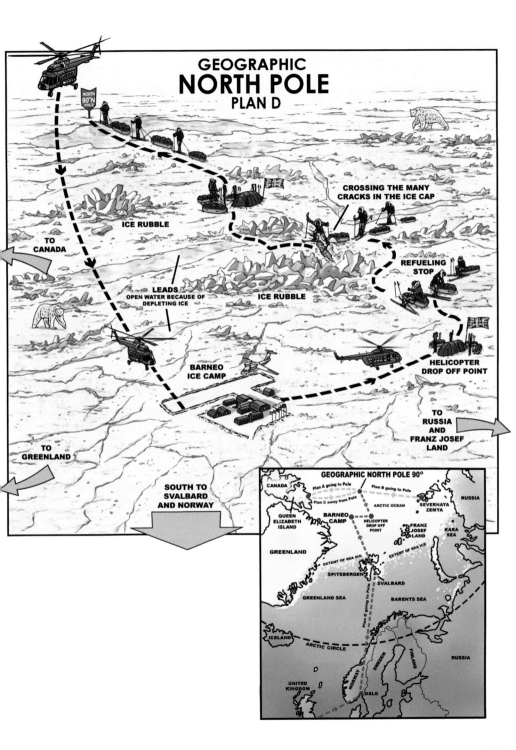

GEOGRAPHIC
NORTH POLE
PLAN D

NORTH 90°N POLE

CROSSING THE MANY CRACKS IN THE ICE CAP

ICE RUBBLE

TO CANADA

REFUELING STOP

LEADS
OPEN WATER BECAUSE OF DEPLETING ICE

ICE RUBBLE

BARNEO ICE CAMP

HELICOPTER DROP OFF POINT

TO RUSSIA AND FRANZ JOSEF LAND

TO GREENLAND

SOUTH TO SVALBARD AND NORWAY

GEOGRAPHIC NORTH POLE 90°

CANADA

Plan A going to Pole

Plan B going to Pole

Plan C away from Pole

ARCTIC OCEAN

RUSSIA

QUEEN ELIZABETH ISLAND

BARNEO CAMP

HELICOPTER DROP OFF POINT

SEVERNAYA ZEMYA

FRANZ JOSEF LAND

KARA SEA

GREENLAND

EXTENT OF SEA ICE

EXTENT OF SEA ICE

SPITSBERGEN

SVALBARD

Plan D going to Pole

GREENLAND SEA

BARENTS SEA

ICELAND

ARCTIC CIRCLE

NORWAY

SWEDEN

FINLAND

RUSSIA

UNITED KINGDOM

OSLO

8th April 2016
Our plan was to meet the Russians again. Viktor and Leo were there and we were updated on the costs [for the last two degrees to the NP], which actually weren't that bad. We agreed with the costs and our priority now was to get back to the pulks and repack them into one larger pulk with 18 days' rations, trimming our kit down. I can't believe that with all the costs, kit and equipment it's come to this!

Later on, we received further bad news after going to another last minute meeting, at which Leo met us rather disturbed saying that there are now problems with the plane getting out!!! Political issues… WTF next!! This is becoming even more frustrating – they said that they would inform us on the situation – I really do not trust the Russians at all!!

When eating into our spare expedition rations, the costs were something we had not accounted for, and we were glad that we had prepared a good budget that included a contingency figure, especially given that Norway is very expensive!

The fact that we had all faced adversities in our lives through past experiences, such as in the military or on previous polar expeditions and in other extreme environments, may have enhanced our resilience for these situations and prevented us from giving up. Our military careers and experiences would have provided a foundation of discipline and a set of shared values. It also meant that we all shared the same sense of humour. This could be quite dark at times, something often required to get through very difficult times!

A joke can often break the ice (excuse the pun!), although it doesn't always work. I remember at a meeting with Mark and a number of polar 'legends' (all with huge egos) who were taking clients to 'walk the last degree', we had a discussion about the runway. The ice was messed up, no one could travel any further, there were massive risks, and it was all so dangerous. At the end of this very serious discussion I piped up and said, "I have one question for everyone here – do they do tea at the North Pole?" My joke didn't go down very well at all! Had there been more British people there, they would have appreciated the idea that there is always room for a cup of tea. Where there's tea there's hope, eh? Good old British spirit! Unfortunately, it was wasted here, and at my expense.

"Will there be tea at the Pole?" Christmas card by John the Brush

<u>10th April 2016</u>
Mark L and myself are keen to get some skiing in – at least do something as we wait This is becoming ridiculous now – we've been here 16 days, moved four times and have been told so many different things that we don't know who or what to believe. I do hope that we can recover something from this and at least do the last two degrees, but even this is looking doubtful.

Later, Viktor, in his usual Russian, charismatic way, explained in a nutshell that we should plan for 17th April – a week away! We just sat, listened and it was 'no change' for us, we will attempt the two degrees!! I did ask Viktor if

they do English Tea at Barneo!? Ha, ha, ha! So, at least we know now and can plan a bit and do some training. And so we retired back to the cabins, looking on the bright side and seeing what tomorrow brings!

The Russians

Our expedition seemed to be dogged by political issues between the UK and Russia, as well as Norway and Russia. It's not clear who the 'baddies' were in all of these situations, but there were certainly some!

As explained previously, earlier on in the process, when we had been planning our final stages of Plan B to travel from the Russian coastline, at the same time the Litvinenko poisoning inquiry had taken place. Suddenly, relationships between the UK and Russia deteriorated, creating political tensions. We managed to obtain our individual visas, but with only three weeks to go until the expedition we had some terrible news. Our group transit visa, an important document for traveling to the coastline through the myriad of checkpoints along the way, was refused. This had been a real blow, on top of which we heard that due to our 'military' links, they had refused us entry.

Further to this, when we arrived in Spitsbergen in Norway, other political issues developed between Norway and Russia. Firstly, a political figure from Russia had been smuggled into Spitsbergen, only to have been spotted and photographed. This caused serious angst between the two countries. To be honest, I was

Press cutting about the Russians parachuting at the North Pole

Russia's Division of Airborne Troops practice airdrops in preparation for an exercise scheduled on an ice floe at the Barneo ice camp this month. The Russian Ministry of Defense said military instructors are planning a stopover at Svalbard Airport as part of the exercise.

RUSSIAN MINISTRY OF DEFENSE

Brash landing

Russia's plans to have military instructors land in Longyearbyen may violate Svalbard Treaty

By MARK SABBATINI
Editor

Russia is planning to have military instructors make a stopover in Longyearbyen as part of a large-scale paratrooper exercise near the North Pole this month, an action that may violate the Svalbard Treaty.

The stopover, first reported by *The Independent Barents Observer*, will involve Russian airborne forces, plus possibly troops from allied countries such as Belarus, Kazakhstan and Armenia. The airdrop onto the Barneo ice camp at 89 degrees north latitude will be followed by exercises in the area, similar to drills Russia has done in the region during the past two years.

"In Moscow they'll assemble platforms for airdrop," a post at the Russian Geographical Society's Expedition Center's Facebook page notes. "The next day these platforms will be transported to Murmansk and loaded with barrels of fuel. Our An-74 will also fly there with the rest of the equipment for the camp, so as

not to make an extra technical flight from Longyearbyen to Barneo. In Murmansk the fuel and equipment will be made ready to be dropped over Barneo. The An-74 will bring to Longyearbyen instructors and dog sledges for the Airborne forces' exercise."

Using Svalbard to prepare for a military exercise may violate a section of the Svalbard Treaty that, according to the Norwegian government's interpretation, states "All foreign military activity in Svalbard is prohibited and would entail a gross infringement of sovereignty."

"Unless they involve innocent passage through territorial waters, foreign military and civilian government vessels wishing to enter Norwegian territorial waters around Svalbard must apply well in advance for diplomatic clearance. The same applies to calls at ports in Svalbard and landings at airports."

Russia deliberately provoked Norway when Deputy Prime Dmitry Rogozin stopped in Longyearbyen and Barentsburg on his way to last year's training exercise. Although he was on Norway's list of banned persons, the restriction didn't apply to Svalbard. Norway subsequently altered entry rules for the archipelago. **There's more!** Visit www.icepeople.net for the complete story.

At a Russian briefing... and not a happy bunny!

never sure what this was all about, but again the political atmosphere had changed, and again it was out of our hands!

Alongside this there were reports (and eventually photographs) in the local paper of Russian troops parachuting into the North Pole, conducting military exercises and flexing their muscles. It was not until we finally reached the ice pole airport that I could confirm a military presence of Russian forces, armed and dressed in camouflage whites. Personally, I think that this also added to our delays, and with the continually cracked runways our opportunity for Plan C (travelling from the pole to Canada) was thwarted, and may never have been a goer anyway.

Either way, the political issues that were created during this time were not at all helpful. They were out of our control and something we had not planned for. Out of interest, there were no expeditions to the North Pole in 2019 due to a dispute between Russia and Ukraine. Prior to the Covid-19 crisis, the 2020 Barneo season had also been postponed due to aircraft problems and disputes between Russia and Ukraine, leading to the Ukrainian authorities refusing use of their aircraft. Now, the pandemic will have its own impact on polar expeditions.

In 1991, 'Victory in Arctic and Antarctic Research' (VICAAR) was set up, specialising in services for adventurous people who want to visit the polar regions, providing key logistical support. From 2018 onwards, Barneo was transferred from Russian control to that of a Swiss company, but it is still run from St Petersburg in Russia.

VICAAR has its base set up near the Pole (wherever they can), consisting of a small tented area with an ice runway. They only stay on ice for a short period, due to the risks of ice fragility and other problems. They try to keep a base open and fly 'tourists' in on their small Antonov plane, and with paying customers handing over Euros this is big business for them. The Russians are very much in control with what seems like a mafia-style business set-up to me.

The evidence of Russian military involvement, with armed soldiers in their Arctic whites at the base station, should lead to questions about why the Russians are taking control of the Arctic and showing force in such a way. In his book, *Prisoners of Geography*, Tim Marshall explains the Russian's increased military presence and how important the region is becoming globally:

Happier times... giving the Russians a bottle of vodka from our sponsors

Russia, meanwhile, is building an Arctic army. Six new military bases are being constructed and several mothballed Cold War installations… are reopening, and airstrips are being renovated. A force of at least 6,000 combat soldiers is being readied for the Murmansk region and will include two mechanised infantry brigades equipped with snowmobiles and hovercraft. (Tim Marshall, *Prisoners of Geography*, 277)

In May 2019, Russia launched a nuclear-powered icebreaker to join a fleet of at least 12 other vessels, as they put into practice ambitious plans to tap the Arctic's commercial potential. Their belief is that the Northern Sea Route will be navigable all year round (which I think it could be – watch this space!), and as they vie for dominance of the Arctic over others such as Canada, USA, Norway and now even China, they wish to hold on to as much power and control in the north as they can.

As Tim Marshall concludes:

When the icemen come, they will come in force. Who has the force? The Russians. No-one else has such a heavy

Why is there an armed Russian soldier welcoming us at Barneo?

presence in the region or is as well prepared to tackle the severity of the conditions. All the other nations are lagging behind. (Tim Marshall, *Prisoners of Geography*, 268.)

Based on this, and with my military training in mind, I feel that the Russians are very much in control and dominant around this region. They not only scuppered our initial plans to the North Pole, but there may be something much larger that we don't know about happening in this region – something strategic and definitely worth keeping an eye on....

6. On Thin Ice!

We are the pilgrims, master; we shall go always a little further: it may be beyond that last blue mountain barred with snow, across that angry or that glimmering sea.

James Elroy Flecker

The irony was that we spent more time in Svalbard than we did on the Arctic Ocean! It's a pretty sad fact which was all down to the climate crisis (and the Russians).

11th April 2016
Mark Wood received a call from Viktor stating that, amazingly, the runway has been sorted and we could be going tomorrow!!!

I sit here in the kitchen of the block with an outstanding view of beauty of the Svalbard mountains – nice!!! Anyway, let's see what happens…. Stay tuned to this Frederick Forsyth saga!!!

After nearly three frustrating weeks, we became optimistic and knew we were close to leaving. We had been given the nod by the Russians that we would be picked up that evening to leave for the airport and travel to Barneo. This was the closest we had been so far, so fingers crossed. That afternoon was spent trying to relax, as well as feeling apprehensive. We had a good feed and performed the final titivations of any kit and equipment. An hour to go and we started to kit up at 2230hrs. With all our gear we were ready to go. Could this be it? I f***ing hoped so!

By the way, it was also my nine-year wedding anniversary. Typical that yet again I wouldn't be there for it but, luckily, I had planned ahead and ordered a nice card and some flowers.

This seems to be the story of my life and I have, unfortunately, missed many an important occasion, mainly due to my busy military career. It's worth noting that having that mutual support from your partner, backing you along the way, is so important and means so much. In fact, our relationship has been built on resilience; it has been tested at times, but it bounces back. The importance of such relationships cannot be understated. We have stood beside each other through thick and thin, even when I volunteered to go to the Poles!

Wearing all our gear in the lodge was hot and I felt like a spaceman going out onto the moon. We went to reception, handed in our keys, paid up and said our goodbyes. The lodge had been great and the owner came and saw us off, handing each of us the gift of a pretty cool hat. I felt that we had become part of the furniture and they knew us fairly well, although I'm not sure if they were sad or happy to see us go.

The van turned up and we loaded all our kit on board for the 20-minute ride to the airport, where there were other expeditions also preparing. There was a hustle and bustle which looked promising, and the small Ukrainian Antonov aircraft was being made ready. We chatted with the other groups, some of whom looked worried and anxious, whilst others tried to look cool, much like people do at the start of a race. We kept to ourselves and started to focus on the mission in hand. We were manhandling our pulks on board the rear of the aircraft, when one of the other expedition guides commented on how heavy our pulks were! Well, it was too late by then, and we had packed everything that was required. We were satisfied, at least.

It seems that sometimes you get comments and advice from so-called 'experts' that actually sow seeds of doubt, but you have to believe in yourself and your own actions. There is no harm in listening and taking some advice, but whether you take it on board or not is another question. We ignored the many comments we received from those 'experts', and everything worked well for us and our team with all our kit and equipment.

Ready to go

12th April 2016
We had to wait around with all the other groups and load
all our kit on the aircraft which was a push, and then
boarded which was a squeeze and very uncomfortable but
we weren't complaining! We were off.

So we boarded the aircraft all kitted up, although we had to take a
few layers off because it was very uncomfortable and hot in all the kit,
and I hate being hot. The plane was full to the brim and we were off!
After a few hours' flying we prepared to land, hitting the ice runway with
a few bumps, but we had landed on the Arctic Ocean. We were here, at
last!

After 2.5hrs, arrived with a bump onto the ice runway – we
were here at Barneo!! It was very cold: -25 to -30°C and we
offloaded all the kit and prepared to go off by hele.

Just landed at Barneo

On arrival, it was approximately 25–30 degrees below zero. There were a few tents and the runway – that was it. Initially, we were ushered into the main tent area, which was guarded by a soldier in camouflage whites. This was a bit bizarre, but the military training exercise that had been reported was a possible explanation. Perhaps the soldier had been injured, or something?

Anyway, we managed to grab a quick brew and chat with other people attempting the last degree (basically, a week on ice). There were all sorts of people waiting there with their own agendas and reasons for attempting to reach the North Pole. Lots of people travel out to the last degree so that they can be the first to do this and that, all pushing themselves on in different ways. We are all different, and we all have different motivations for why we push and ideas about what we aim for, all of which can be admired in their own right. We then retired into a corner to enjoy our final cup of tea (they do make tea at the Pole!).

We were soon called back out and MW received a briefing. We packed the necessary fuel onto our pulks because the large Russian cargo helicopters had arrived to take us straight to our drop off point.

A cup of tea in Barneo before we left

Along with two other groups, we loaded our heavy pulks onto the Russian helicopter and geared up for take-off. It was all a bit surreal. Outside was still daylight, but by now we were heading into the early hours of the morning and were feeling a bit weary. We took off and sped above the ice. On looking down, all we could see was a thin white sheet, rough with cracks in many places, as well as large expanses of open water. We hoped and prayed that we could land safely.

After about an hour, we set the first two groups down at the last degree. We shook their hands and then took off again, looking at their small specks on the ground. Their expedition had just started and now, after three years of planning and hardships, we were about to begin ours. After a further hour we landed again. This was our turn. We unloaded, shook hands, and the helicopter heated up for take-off.

I could not resist putting the British flag up and waving it at the Ruskies as they took off. I wasn't sure what they thought of us 'crazy' Brits, but I simply wanted to make the point that this was us, a British expedition, and after three years we are going to make this happen – see you later Russians! I felt that this was actually a moment of success

The helicopter that was to drop us off at 88°

and elation, just to finally be on the Arctic Ocean. We had made it this far, after such a long journey faced with many obstacles. I knew that once we were on ice we would manage and make it work as a team.

We loaded ourselves onto the hele with all our kit. Off we took until it was our DOP, 88° – dropped off and we moved off. It was about 8 in the morning, so we immediately pitched tent, planting the Union Jack. Meanwhile, the Russians were fuelling up the hele and watching (and filming) us. They then lifted off and we were left on our own – three years in the making and we were on the Arctic ice!! Hooray!!

As it was late, we decided to pitch the tent straight away, get some sleep and then start first thing. Unfortunately, my feet were very cold and the one thing you find when you try to sleep with cold feet is that you can't! Sleep is so important and is often underestimated. It is vital for recovery both physically and psychologically.

We set up the tent and kit like clockwork, just as we had rehearsed relentlessly during our preparations. We each knew what to do, and the last thing we needed was for the tent to blow away. We were exhilarated and excited about being there, and confident in our ability to do this.

It is important when doing any form of endurance event or expedition of this sort that you make a progressive and steady start. It's not a race, and those who act as if it is will be unlikely to make it to their finish point in one piece. Anyway, we were there, and we chatted briefly, discussing what time to be underway. This was our first night on the Arctic Ocean – quite an exciting but anxious moment! Initially, sleeping on ice was a bit of a worry, as you hear stories about falling through the ice all wrapped up in a tent! Sadly, earlier in that year there were some scientists conducting some scientific research on the ice sheet near Canada who did exactly that.

We had about six hours' rest and were up to start at 1400hrs (ready to leave for 1600hrs) for our first day on ice. Routine was key. Routine is a critical part in all our lives in coping and getting through the day. Without routine we would not get anywhere!

Routine

On our expedition, routine helped enormously as we chipped away at the miles every day in the attempt to reach our goal. I love routine, and coming from the military this is indoctrinated into you – and it works! From getting up in the morning (reveille) to when we eat and go to bed – it is all planned. This is even more important when on ice, as without routine you would get nowhere. Routine is so important because it:

- enables you to get through the day, sometimes dragging you through it!
- helps you to achieve goals and tasks, getting you from A to B
- provides structure
- provides rhythm and security
- provides a sense of order and organisation
- enables everyone to know what they are doing
- builds good habits
- increases efficiency and productivity

So our routine in the North Pole could be broken down into four parts, a bit like your normal day:

1. Get up! Morning routine (2 hours)
2. Ski routine (6–12 hours) – this is your day routine
3. Tent routine (3–4 hours)
4. Sleep routine (8–10hours)

SKI ROUTINE

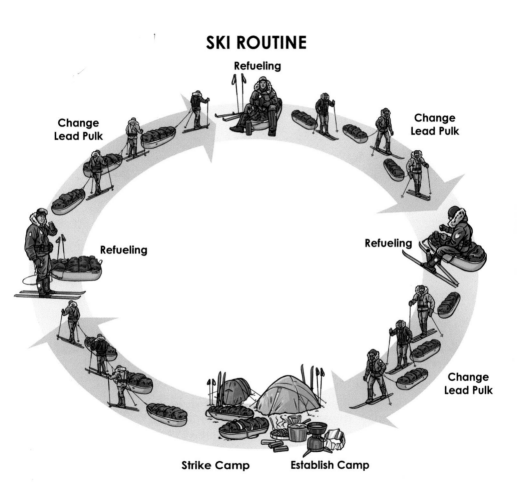

Refueling

Change Lead Pulk

Change Lead Pulk

Refueling

Refueling

Change Lead Pulk

Strike Camp

Establish Camp

TENT ROUTINE

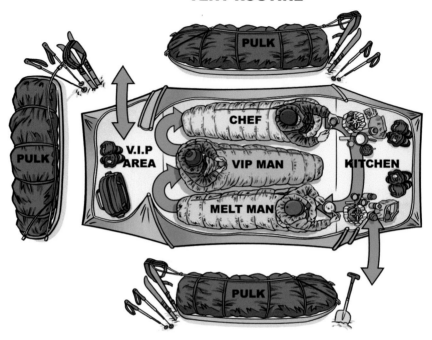

It started with the morning routine where, as three men crammed in a tent, one would be boiling the ice, acting as 'melt man', with another then pouring the melted water into the kettle to prepare our high-calorie expedition food and drink, acting as 'the chef'. At the same time, the third person was chilling and doing his own admin – he was the 'VIP man' for that day. These job roles were then rotated daily so that every two days you would look forward to being the VIP. All of this preparation took about two hours every morning, but it was an important ritual necessary for a successful day ahead.

It's worth mentioning that getting up in the morning could sometimes be a struggle. Firstly, opening up the warm folds of your sleeping bag to the freezing cold and having to get up and get going is quite a challenge. This, mixed with the aches and pains of the previous day, in addition to the mental worries and anxieties about what may lay ahead, made getting out of bed the first test of the day!

Once breakfast and flasks were complete, next it was a matter of putting kit away, packing up our sleeping bags, brushing teeth, maybe a visit to the toilet, and kitting up. Boots on and we were good to go! Outside, and a slick collapse of the tent as a team, rolling it back up and inserting it into the bag, so that it could be unrolled just as easily at the end of the day. Then, load the pulks back up with our kit, put on our harnesses, check our bearings as a team and then we were off!

Clothing

Clothing and being properly dressed is critical when operating in extreme regions. Firstly, you do not want to overheat and start sweating, because sweat turns cold and becomes ice, cooling you down and making you extremely cold and unable to operate, which can then lead to hypothermia. You need to protect your whole body, including your head, hands and face, from the elements. The cold will find any nook and cranny, it does not take any prisoners!

Taking gloves off for longer than a minute or two to do something, such as opening your flask or taking down the tent, could potentially cause problems, from frostnip to frostbite. There have been many times when my hands have told me that I have left my gloves off for too long! The tell-tale signs of losing functionality of the fingers, followed by warming up and the associated pain of blood recirculating, sometimes left me in tears, shouting out in pain (which was, thankfully, muffled by the poor weather).

The warmest protection for the hands is actually a mitten with internal touch gloves so that you don't get caught out with the cold. Having a mitten provides the greatest warmth as your fingers are together and create heat, unlike a normal glove. However, you still need to do things which require dexterity, and a mitten can be cumbersome and frustrating when trying to do even simple tasks, such as undoing a zip. So, having an internal glove is recommended as it allows you to take off your mitten briefly, providing some initial protection, and then hopefully put the mitten back on in time. However, some clever designers have now come up with a hybrid-type glove which is more of a mitten, with the trigger finger free to move, giving greater dexterity. I would recommend these, and also doing some training at home, doing household chores wearing mittens! So, the 'spork' kind of mitten, with a thumb and forefinger, is the best option because it affords some dexterity. As I say, you do need to conduct some functional operations, such as taking out tent pegs or opening a packet of pork scratchings.

You really cannot afford to mess about, and your administration has to be shit hot, otherwise you will be punished by the cold. Many others have been caught out with lifelong injuries, but good organisation means that this should just not be happening. If you can return unscathed, it is one measure of the success of the mission.

Out on ice we also had a number of different gloves, mittens, hats and balaclavas to accommodate the different conditions and situations, and also for back-up. By the way, having a beard in the polar regions is actually not practical, because it can stick to the inside of your balaclava and removing hair with skin can be excruciatingly painful. It may look cool in the pictures, but it is not actually recommended!

On my feet I wore Alfa North Pole specialist boots, three sizes too big, to allow room for all of my socks. I wore a thin pair, followed by waterproof-type socks to capture sweat (a bit like a carrier-bag), then large 'bad-boy' thick socks which were inserted into the boot with a bit of a squash and a squeeze. These boots were very good, having worn them for 76 days in the South, hence they were broken-in and moulded to my feet. It is vital to have broken-in boots.

There is nothing worse than blisters, although, of course, we had to be prepared for them, even with broken-in boots. Blisters can be debilitating, and even the smallest of blisters can slow you down so are something you cannot afford to have. With anything medical, I would always try to advise that prevention is better than cure, and this also applies to blisters. So if you have any hot spots, places that are rubbing, Compeed and tape them up. I actually had a blister on the plateau of the South Pole and had to stop. Doing this in -40oC is not fun, but it was necessary.

Luckily, I always have my medical pack on standby for these types of situations – for myself and for the team.

On my legs I wore my ski trousers which have followed me through my skiing, alpine, and ski touring life. I have patched them up several times and they are still good-to-go today. Suitable ski pants need adequate venting, as well as good pockets. I have also added small, extra lanyard loops to all of my zips to ensure ease of access to pockets when wearing gloves in the cold, particularly when going to the toilet!

I layered up with a Lifa thermal vest, fairly thick with a ¾ zip at the top for venting. The last bit of clothing, and the most important, was of course the jacket, which had to be weather-resistant, particularly giving protection from the severe wind. Added to this was a water-resistant cotton-style smock (an old smock also works, and ML used one in the South). This time, I invested in a Fjallraven G1000 specialist smock, a beast of a jacket, and I have to say it worked well for these environments (as you can see in the pictures of me wearing it).

Properly layered up for the extreme conditions

It was so good to be back on ice. At the beginning, the ice felt a bit like polystyrene and the texture was much different to that in the Antarctic. In fact, it was very different for a whole manner of reasons. We were on a fragile ocean, to start with! The top layer of the ice contained the salt of the sea (so we had to be careful when using the snow to melt for cooking). At the South Pole I had encountered a variety of snow conditions: sticky, thick, wet, crevassed and sastrugi, all of which were challenging. Sastrugi means 'wave' and are the frozen waves of the ocean. They can be a real frustration, and constantly dragging pulks up and over these takes its toll, physically and mentally. In the North, the floating ice sheet consisted of many obstacles, including ice rubble, walls of ice, thin ice, thick ice, etc. It was all different, and changed constantly just to challenge us, or so it seemed!

To be honest, if we had been on ice for the same length of time as we had been during the South Pole expedition (76 days), I don't know whether we would have made it, simply because the conditions were so much more demanding and relentless. In the South we had been faced with obstacles, but it wasn't always as relentless, whereas in the North it was a real challenge. Plus, in the South we were pulling 160kg in one long pulk, and not 80kg as we were in the North – although pulling 80kg actually felt more like 160kg over that terrain.

Given the different conditions, we had to adjust our plans. Initially, we were going to proceed hauling two pulks. However, hauling two smaller pulks in those conditions would have been horrendous, so we were glad to drop down to one.

Punching through the Arctic Ocean ice

The ice is different here compared to the South – hard snow
with some thin snow, ice underneath – the Arctic Ocean.

To be totally honest, the three of us were a very slick team on ice! We were like a train determined to reach its destination on time. We literally forced our way through ice rubble, across open leads, and over the maze of ice that we came across. We pushed through and made progress with an efficiency and determination that was reassuring – plenty of PESTO!

13th April 2016
A cold day (-20 to -25°C), we set off on our bearing North
(280°) and decided to do 2 x 1hr stints taking us until late;
a total of 6hrs marching (7hrs in total with rests). The weights
of our sledges are 80kg and feel like a dead weight when
pulling – very hard going even over the smaller bumps.
'Back-breaking' work I feel, and is very hard physically and
endurance-wise – but doable at least. You definitely need
snacks every hour to keep you going.

The Russians were constantly putting us under pressure, asking us every day over the radio whether we would make a particular distance. They pushed us as far as they could, warning that a weather front was on its way, demanding that we reach a specific point by a specific time. At the end of each day, when we had to radio in and tell them our coordinates, they would be saying all sorts of things to try and quicken our pace. All the time we were thinking and saying amongst ourselves, "Give it a rest, we are busting our guts out here to make the distance." Their pressure was relentless, in a very negative way. Thankfully, that didn't put us off and we just thought, *Oh the Russians!* Did it drive us further? It might have given us the bit between our teeth to keep us going, that's for sure.

A 'take-home' here is to be in control of what you *can* control, and not to worry about what is out of your control. This applied to us throughout the expedition with regard to the environment, as well as those damn Ruskies!

We couldn't afford to have a day of rest, even if it was required, as we had to keep moving and make the most of the available time to get to the Geographic North Pole. There were long days on the ice. Our routine grew more streamlined with every passing day. As with any environment that you are faced with, your initial reaction is to question and ask, "What is all this about?" Yet within a short time we had worked out our system, developing the basics of setting up the tent and our daily routine, drawing on what we had established during the South Pole expedition and our training.

To be honest, our minds were so distracted during the whole expedition, it was all very intense. With everything that we were facing, from the obstacles of ice, cracks (leads), thin ice, polar bear threat and travelling as far as we could in the correct direction every day, we were being tested mentally and physically throughout. It was a bit like being in a maze and having to find your way through it. When our minds weren't busy, we were resting or asleep, preparing for the next day. This was unlike the South Pole, where we sometimes had time to think and drift off.

14th April 2016
We packed the tent up and it was a glorious day in the Arctic
– like a different planet here. It was unnaturally hot and we
had to reduce down to two Lifa vests – hot work. Initially,
going went well until we hit large ice blocks and a lead to
cross which was sapping work and hard pulling. It really is
hard pulling, straining our backs over all this rubble.

Nevertheless, the experience in the South and our training could not prepare us fully for the environment of the North Pole. I still maintain that this environment is the harshest one known to humans, especially with climate change and the way the ice is breaking up. It creates an enormously challenging terrain. Every few hundred metres we were faced with walls of ice rubble. This is where ice crashes into other ocean ice and rides up, creating more ice rising up yet further. We would have to climb over these huge barricades. They were not thin layers of ice, but boulders of huge thick ice blocks which we had to find our way through, looking for the weakest point and creating a route over the rubble. This could involve removing our skis, securing them to the pulk, and then manhauling the pulk over a wall of ice, all the time being

Climbing over ice rubble

careful not to injure ourselves or damage our equipment. This all took time and had to be done properly. Sometimes we hit double walls, or we were faced with walls all around us! I remember one time we had penetrated the initial four or five walls of ice only to find that we were surrounded and trapped in a small football pitch sized area, and then we lost the sun! In my mind it was like being trapped inside a castle made of ice. My heart sank on several occasions and sometimes I wondered whether we would ever get through it! However, through some PESTO and perseverance we punched through our obstacles and whatever the environment was throwing at us. We realised that, as a team, we had the confidence to overcome all of these challenges.

> _16th April 2016_
> _Had a rough night's sleep last night, but got up and on with the usual routine as 'melt man'. Woke up cold, but knew we just had to get on, which we all did and were ready to go shortly after 10am._
> _The environment became very messy, with ice rubble and loads of open leads. Except this time the leads were full of thin ice and very dodgy to cross. Mark L nearly fell in after an edge broke and he did a pirouette managing to balance – what a legend. We continued on, very hard going, the hardest yet, and we were faced with steam, showing large areas of sea ice and water – this was becoming dodgy! [Steam occurs where the water in open leads is heated by the sun.] We meandered and weaved our way through what we came up against, making some good calls I thought. It really is a maze out here and very hard work, especially with the weight of the pulks behind us – manhandling at times – not easy. We crossed massive disturbance, rubble and ice blocks. I hope this gets a lot easier._

All this had to be done as an efficient team. The obstacles that the ice threw at us were relentless and it must have been similar to crossing enemy territory during the war, facing trenches, then barbed wire, then a mine field, then hedges, then more wire. This relentlessness inevitably had an effect on us psychologically, sapping our physical and mental power.

We were constantly being tested and put under pressure, and sometimes stress, which created elements of fear. There were a few times when I thought about 'fear', but having been exposed to this during my military career, it hadn't crippled me or our team in the South Pole. I guess this could be quite different if you were on your own, faced with just your own thoughts and doubts, with no-one to bounce ideas off or drag you along on your bad days. That's why working as a team is by far the safer option and provides that small respite, socialisation and support – especially important when you're isolated with risks all around you.

In addition, we might be faced with a large open lead of water caused by the ice breaking open. Often, we decided that, where possible, we would go around the water, rather than face all the hassle of putting on our dry bags, etc, which added time that we didn't really have. Our research and preparation had told us that more often than not you could find a place to cross and, eventually, we would. At times we tentatively crossed ice as it broke around us. I remember some occasions where MW literally had ice bowing under his feet, seconds away from falling through into the icy water. It's funny because Captain Scott mentioned falling into crevasses during his South Pole expedition, and that he became so exposed and actually excited at the thought of these risks, it would have actually built his resilience. The fact is, you do become acclimatised and resilient to your environment. Sometimes, walking miles around these obstacles also played on our mental resilience, which could be very frustrating, so trying to cross them was sometimes a much more attractive but riskier affair. We were also taking risks due to time pressure and the Russians hassling us – bloody Russians again!

17th April 2016
We continued on bearing only to find ourselves at a very large expanse of water, with the usual rubble and ice leads – great!! So we skirted around, crossing some dodgy leads, one of which Mark W stood on and it bowed. We got around and back on bearing but it took a massive amount of time.

I was on next and, guess what, even worse. We went into another area, except this time a lot closer to the water and it was moving all the ice right in front of our eyes – it made a sound, gurgling, and the ice was getting crushed up – very scary!! One time, the ice cracked around us and drifted apart,

Crossing an open water lead

and Mark W had to jump over. We decided to get out of there
and boxed around for quite a distance just to avoid it all.

The walls of ice sometimes led us into an ice maze, much like those hedge mazes you see at stately homes, although much more fearsome and dangerous! So we had to weave our way around and through them, and if we found a dead end, retrace our steps and start again. Such hampered progress could be mentally challenging, sucking out our spirit and optimism, but we just had to summon the strength to think that we would get through this, and have the confidence that we would find a way and, reassuringly as a team, we always did.

18th April 2016
Initially, we made good speed – saying good speed – as fast as you can pulling a heavy pulk (slightly lighter now), climbing all the sastrugi and bumps and climbs. But this was not to be as we hit loads of ice rubble, which was continuous, and we had to climb over it.

We had a few falls, nothing too serious, but there is potential for a serious minor injury to occur.

We continued on, and yes, yet again we were faced by more walls of ice, like battlements to a castle, and we weaved our way through and around. Our physical and mental levels towards the end were slowly being sapped and we managed to make it to a clearer area – thank God. This is where we sit now, comfortable in our tent with sore muscles and backs! Ready for another day. We have, though, managed to make 9.5NM which, considering, is very good. We spoke to the Russians on our daily schedule at 8pm, to be told that Barneo Ice Station is looking at closing on 25th April – so we really are on a Race Against Time!!

The weather was warmer than we had expected, hence the disruption and problems with fractured ice. One morning, we woke up in our tent and it was literally dripping with condensation, such that we had to strip off to our lowest clothing levels. This was a bizarre experience because we were used to being all wrapped up against the cold. What on earth was happening out there?

Navigation

Navigating in any polar region can be tremendously difficult, due to the extreme weather fronts, constant whiteouts and the impact of working close to the Poles. Having had to navigate my way throughout my military career in a number of different countries and environments, plus having taught guys in the military the art of navigation, being a military navigation instructor myself, it is second nature to me in normal circumstances. However, when faced with extreme environments, the cold, poor weather and visibility, everything seems totally different and much more difficult. I have had to use rocks, clouds, the sun and spindrift to help me gauge my direction whilst still moving. This is an art.

Whiteouts, in layman's terms, are when the sky meets the ground and your whole visual field is just 'white', such that you lose sight of anything which might help you get a navigational fix. They have been described as being inside a ping-pong ball, and to me it's like navigating on some bizarre film set with just a white background! The Pathfinder struggles to get his fix and sometimes drifts left and right, and in really bad conditions you can simply go round and round in circles. It is often the guy at the back who sees this happening, so calls a stop and corrects the leader, although it can be very frustrating to have a back-seat driver telling you where to go!

To be honest it is something I dread, and no doubt others hate, as the whiteouts hinder progress terribly and can even cause you to stop and sometimes set up camp. Perhaps we can all relate this to events in life when we need to get going, but something is simply slowing us down, such as being stuck in traffic or behind a tractor (all day) and needing to get to an important meeting. Well, a whiteout is just like that, but for prolonged periods of time, possibly days.

So, how do we navigate? The most important piece of equipment is a proven, calibrated compass for the Northern Hemisphere which is trustworthy – the type of compass that flips open with a mirror on the other side (which is also handy for checking whether you have any frostbite),

bought at reputable outdoor shops. (I purchased mine in Oslo for this trip.) The next issue is how to hold the compass whilst you are skiing with a ski pole in each arm, and for this you need some kind of level holder. I used my parachuting compass holder, which is a fabric body harness which unzips and releases the compass all ready to use in front of me! Of course, a hundred years ago our ancestors used a sextant which took a massive amount of time and effort, requiring a level surface, often meaning that they had to lie on the frozen ground to take a bearing, all of which took valuable time.

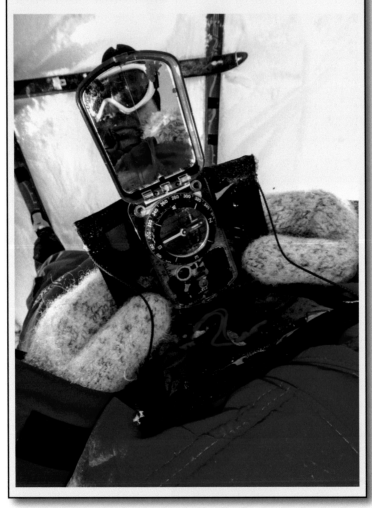

So what about modern technology and GPS? Well, they have their place, but the severe cold environment creates problems holding these items and actually using the buttons, as well as affecting and draining the batteries in them (which is where solar power steps in). We usually checked the GPS at the end of the day (to confirm location and daily mileage), and also towards the end of the trip when we were nearer the Pole to ensure we were on bearing. A normal compass starts to do some crazy things as you approach the Poles, so at this stage reliance on GPS increases.

For the North Pole we had also been given some great watches by SUUNTO. Initially, I was slightly sceptical about these because I like a simple watch powered by kinetic energy, preferring not to rely on external power, whereas these watches would run out of power about every two weeks, requiring solar charging as we went along. However, this watch was a god-send because when we consulted it in the morning, we could take a location reading (which would inform us whether we had drifted overnight in the right direction), as well as confirming when we actually got to the Geographic North Pole. The watch also had a number of other great gadgets which helped us, such as a storm alarm and an altimeter, for example. I highly recommended the watch and I still wear it today, although no doubt the model has now been upgraded and, of course, there are others on the market. Shop wisely and get to know how to use your equipment.

In terms of weather, the sun was, of course, our friend. We knew how to navigate using it, but when it disappeared, crossing those obstacles became even more challenging. Then, the world became a cold, dark, horrible and very lonely place. At one moment the sun is showing you the way and then, all of a sudden, you are plunged into darkness physically and emotionally as everything becomes colder, turning the canvas to a black and white world.

The sun is your biggest friend in the polar regions, and up in the Arctic it aids you with navigation as well as providing you with your own shadow which you can lock onto, thus lessening the need to check your compass all of the time. For example, at 1000hrs, my own shadow was on my left, at about 7 o'clock, and would start to move to the 8 o'clock position during my shift. So, as long as I kept the shadow at that angle, I would remain on my set bearing without needing to check my compass all the time.

The sun also provides definition on the ground so that you can work out the depth of an object, which is especially helpful when crossing over boulders and ice rubble. We had a few occasions when the sun disappeared and it became increasingly difficult to navigate. This was frustrating, particularly when you are falling over and constantly sapping your energy reserves. When the sun is hidden by clouds, it also becomes very cold, bringing the temperature down by at least 5-10 degrees, a change which nearly caught me out on a few occasions.

On Wednesday 27th December 1911 Captain Scott wrote:

> *We have lost sight of the sun since we came to the summit; we should get an extraordinary record of sunshine. It is monotonous work; this sledgemeter (measures distance) and theodolite (equipment to assist with angles, direction and used for land survey) govern the situation.*

Polar Bears

We had two instances when we saw evidence of polar bears. The first was on day four or five when, stepping out of the tent in the morning, we saw these huge polar bear footprints about 300–400 metres away. The tracks were massive, quite literally 'big foot', and we had to comprehend the sheer size and the fact that they were not far from our tent! I'll be honest and admit this caused some worry, and for a while the hairs stood up on the back of my neck. However, we had to get on with the job and not worry about this, and we were soon back to normal speed.

Two days later we were walking along and discovered more polar bear footprints passing our track, together with some smaller prints (perhaps an Arctic Fox, as they often follow along with the bears to scavenge their scraps). Luckily, we never got to see a polar bear, but they could have easily been watching us, following us, and getting ready to investigate, we just didn't know. As I have mentioned, we were prepared. ML had a rifle, I had a flare gun, and MW had some firecrackers. In an emergency we would have had to defend against a threatening bear, but we really did not want to do this as it would actually be detrimental to the expedition, to us and to what we were trying to achieve. The ideal method to deal with the threat of bears is to avoid, monitor, and observe them, leaving time to decide what action to take. Whatever happens, it's best to remember that you certainly cannot out-run polar bears, which can track humans from over 20 miles away using their amazing predatory sense of smell.

Polar bear footprints

19th April 2016
Just a few general reflections after a week. It's like another
planet here, on which humans are not meant to be. There is
an air of beauty here as well and on a couple of occasions
have been blown away by its beauty (especially at the end
of the day in the sun). All-in-all, an experience not to be
missed, but I'm glad that we'll be out of here soon – 25th at
the Pole? Fingers crossed.

Walking on ice, despite being together as a team, can make you feel alone with your own thoughts. We had to be mindful of the psychological effects of operating in those conditions, especially in extreme weather when things do not always go to plan and your mind and ability to operate can be seriously hindered. The daily grind of walking hour after hour in what seemed like an identical, never-changing landscape, a 'white treadmill', played on our minds, even though the North Pole and the Arctic are a bit more varied and challenging. We had to overcome this using coping strategies. There was a lot of stuff going on in our heads, but in my experience, that could be used as a strength to reframe our situation in a more positive way, particularly when things became very difficult.

So, for example, although I knew I was in an extremely cold place, I would focus my mind on warmer climes and the time when I got married in St Lucia. By doing this I brought my mind to a warmer, more pleasant experience. Due to the fact that my wife and I were expecting our third child at the time of the expedition, babies names were much on my mind, and thinking through these was a helpful distraction. I would also think about work, life, big things, small things, trivial subjects, financial matters, etc. Having said all that, the constant challenge of the ice, the rubble, the walls and the open leads didn't, in fact, give us much time to drift away into our own thoughts for that long – quite unlike the South Pole experience.

Henry Worsley had told me that to help him mentally he used powerful mantras, such as Lord Tennyson's, recognised in the polar world: "To strive, to seek, to find and not to yield." These words gave him strength with each word, as he used them as a powerful mantra for each stride. My skis had the image of Roald Amundsen painted on them, whereas some people have their children's hand prints on them and other inspirational words – images and ideas that you can look down at as a constant reminder right in front of you, a power to keep you pressing on, and an anchor to keep you focused.

Captain Scott wrote on Wednesday 27th December 1911:

> *One cannot allow one's thoughts to wander as others do, and when, as this afternoon, one gets amongst disturbances, I find it is very worrying and tiring. I do trust we shall have no more of them.*

My skis with the image of Roald Amundsen

The other key focus for me when on an expedition is music. In the South Pole I had one iPod, but this time for the North I bought two small ones, because I wasn't sure that their limit of 500 songs would be enough. They were small, simple gadgets without a screen, and I would walk along wearing one earpiece, keeping the other ear free to listen out for any dangers. Enjoying my eclectic collection such as Pink Floyd, Duran Duran (their song 'This Is Planet Earth') and Muse in such a magical place was incredibly powerful, and music is also powerful as a distraction. I remember that if I heard a low battery signal on the iPod, I could become really glum because I knew that meant I had half an hour's worth of music left. When the music runs out, you are, quite literally, on your own. Some expedition members do not use music, and some were envious, but each to their own. Whatever your personal preference, it's a great distraction for me, and I loved it and got great strength from it.

However, music wasn't always a blessing. I recall one incident when I couldn't get to my iPod to turn off a particular song because I was having to deal immediately with difficult navigation and terrain. The tune that kept ringing in my ear was 'Ebony and Ivory' by Paul McCartney and Stevie Wonder, a song that was very odd for that moment, and one that I am no longer that fond of! Walking in the white environment does encourage you to listen to songs in a deeper way, appreciating words that appear to have more direct and immediate meaning for you. Johnny Cash and the War of the Worlds are examples of some tunes that gave me strength and meaning, increased positivity and power, as I thought that their words and lyrics were written exclusively and purposefully just for me – although, of course, they were not!

> No-one would have believed in the early years of the 19th century that polar affairs were being watched from the timeless worlds of the media.
> No-one could have dreamed that they were being scrutinised as someone with a microscope studies creatures that swarm and multiply with a drop of water.
> Few men even consider the possibility of life in Antarctica.
> And yet, across the Ross Sea, those minds immeasurably superior to ours, regarded this land with envious eyes and slowly, but surely, they drew there plans to the South Pole!

20th April 2016
It went on and on – ice rubble, walls of it as high as houses.
We entered the battlements of the ice castle and into the
breach hoping to punch our way through, only to be stopped
in our tracks with high ice walls which we had to get over –
this was a nightmare!! Both physically and mentally draining,
pulling our pulks over these defences. It became ridiculous
and it seemed it would never stop. At one stage we were in
a small, open space of ground surrounded by ice!!

Then the lights went out! The sun became hidden by a
thick blanket of snow clouds and everything became more
difficult – no sense of perception, navigation nightmare –
what else!? We continued slowly, trying to find a way out of
this puzzle palace. In my mind thinking it might be better to
sit it out in the tent, but we continued. Eventually, after many
hours of hard work and perseverance we popped out into a
better area and guess what – the sun started to appear!

On any expedition where you are facing challenges, difficulties, and isolation in an extreme environment, the question of how you manage your thoughts is key. It's how you manage that third person, the inner person, and how you control him or her. The last thing you want to think about is the pain, the sweat, the cold and the crisis. You need to be in the present to deal with the situation, but also in the future to pull yourself forward. Faced with a white treadmill and a constant relentless hourly trudge, you have to think about something constructive. It's unhelpful to become disheartened, so you need to think about positives, including what you are missing and what you are looking forward to when it all ends. Ernest Shackleton described the belief that an incorporeal person joined him and his small team on the final leg of their journey south. He wrote:

> *When I look back at those days, I have no doubt that*
> *Providence guided us, not only across those snow fields, but*
> *across the storm-white sea… I know that during that long*
> *and racking march of 36 hours over the unnamed mountains*
> *and glaciers of South Georgia it seemed to me often that we*
> *were four, not three. I said nothing to my companions on*

the point, but afterwards Worsley said to me, 'Boss, I had a curious feeling on the march that there was another person with us.' Crean confessed to the same idea.

The Third Man factor is that feeling Shackleton describes, an unseen spirit or companion. It often seems to happen to explorers and travellers who have reached the grimmest peaks of desperation. Since he published his belief, other survivors of extreme conditions have shared similar experiences, and the 'Third Man factor' has become a common expression. This is something I have witnessed on only a few occasions and very few people ever get to experience this feeling.

I experienced most of my fear when we were trying to find a way through the ice rubble. I can only describe it as being in the centre of the earth, like a volcano – the ice behaves almost like hot lava, at the heart of an eruption. We heard ice crushing and cracking and splitting and spurting all around us, water coming up and exploding through the ice, as we were quickly sucked into the centre of the maelstrom. At one

moment we just managed to get out in the nick of time, as Mark Wood jumped across a break in the ice – something which was quite comical but also very serious. As we moved past it the ice crushed up. I recalled the saws spinning and the floors moving in an old fairground funhouse, but with less of the fun element! Think of Indiana Jones as he tries to escape the dissolving temple with its poisoned darts, disappearing floors, rolling balls of stone and swinging saws! This was us, although on the Arctic Ocean in the middle of nowhere! Bizarre, but this is what's happening out there.

The mind is by the far the most powerful motivator and influencer in deciding whether you are successful or not. It really is mind over matter. In an iceberg analogy, the mountain of ice above the water is the 'physical' you and what lies beneath the water and what matters is you, your mind and your emotions – your mental health! It's quite literally what is below the iceberg that matters!

Staying positive, even in the worst conditions and environments, is key to success and survival, and you do not have to be an Arctic explorer to benefit from this wisdom. We hear it so many times, but believe me, it is true and comes to the fore in the most difficult of conditions. Use it to your advantage – never negatively. The mind is a very powerful weapon, particularly when in the right hands.

One of our key positive experiences was the daily use of our pipes. That moment of 'pans away, pipes out' after cooking the evening meal was the time when we allowed ourselves to chat to each other. Explorers a century ago did the same, the action becoming part of their (and our) well-being, creating something special to look forward to. During the day, the smell of tobacco in our balaclavas reminded us about the end of the day, being in a warm tent, having food, and climbing into our sleeping bags. All of these daily rituals to look forward to could be conjured up by the aroma and image of our pipes, helping us get through the day. (It goes without saying that pipe-smoking is not without health dangers, but for a short period we embraced the habit to get us through a larger danger – there were worse current threats!)

21st April 2016
A very cold day today, due to a very strong southerly wind (approx. 15kmh) making it cold, approx. -30°C. Had cold hands today – not nice and had to put my big mitts on – which worked.

THE WHITE TREADMILL
Caterpillar Technique

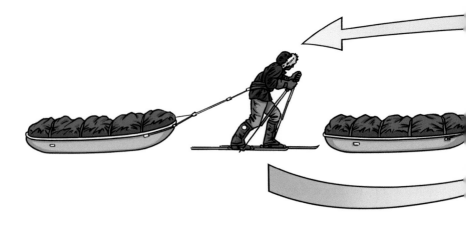

A long drag of a day really, completing over 9hrs on skis and looking forward to the warmth of the tent and hot food. But we had made great progress, covering 11NM (our record so far!) and we are now only 39NM from the Pole – fingers crossed, we should be there on the 25th! The Russians have pushed us again to get picked up for the 25th (pm) – we'll see how we get on… so far so good.

During the day, we would have perhaps seven hours skiing on ice, not including breaks. As we progressed like a small human caterpillar, every hour the person leading would use arm signals to indicate what was to happen. A pole in the air meant a five-minute break, during which we wouldn't talk much, maybe take some film footage and, most importantly, take in some nutrition from our 'nutty bags' (pork scratchings or nuts), and fluids for rehydration. Then we would be back on our way with someone else leading, and we would do the same again, and the same again after that. The next day we might increase the time skiing by 30 minutes, just to push ourselves that little bit further – always a little further.

Swapping lead would take place around every hour and followed by a break.

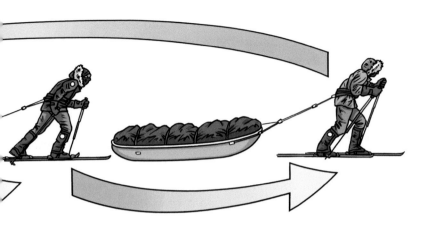

Perhaps most crucial to any endurance event is the need to start progressively, to build up as you go along, and match your activity with the correct nutrition. So initially, when we first landed on ice, we had to match our nutrition with that first effort. This might have meant having just one 800-calorie meal each day for the first week, but then as we increased the time and the mileage, burning more calories, we would then boost the nutrition intake to two main meals (1,600 calories) with perhaps a dessert. By this time, our bodies were craving all the salts, savouries, and calories that they could get. This progression is a pyramid-style method of building up exertion and intake whilst on ice. We could not start out on the first day skiing our maximum distance, flogging ourselves. This was an endurance event, and we had to make sure that we could finish in one piece, by pacing ourselves.

At the end of the day we always checked the distance covered after having our evening meal. With the map and GPS we could discover how far we had gone, and then in our call to base we would give that grid reference to the Russians. This reporting in at the end of the day could be a high point or a low point, depending on the distance we had covered and the attitude of the Russians! We had a set distance of 12 or

13 nautical miles to cover per day, out of our total of 150, so we had to complete the distance in the available time. Barneo Station was lifting off and the Russians were set to go anyway due to the risk on the ice and their worries about their own safety. They were also worried for us and, of course, they wanted to get their money and leave. As a result, the evening reports would be quite negative when we had covered fewer miles during that day, having some psychological effect, but not letting it get us down.

> *23rd April 2016*
>
> *Awoke to a bizarrely hot day here, with the ice in the tent melting… this is strange and the sun was out. So off we went with the sun, until it started to diminish – oh no, not again – the sun really is our friend here, and without it, it makes things difficult – difficult to get depth of perception and navigation.*
>
> *I must say that my iPod is a godsend out here, but already I'm bored of it. Stevie Wonder, Pink Floyd, Phil Collins, Muse and Depeche Mode – what a mix!! Towards the end of the day, still in darkness, we hit another massive expanse of open water (not frozen) and found a place to cross – a bit dodgy but all good. This seems bizarre that only 20 miles from the Pole there is water!! Is this climate change??*

With all of the hours spent on the 'white treadmill', it was important to take our minds away from the situation, for which we had many techniques. However, as in the South Pole, humour played a key role in coping with our adverse conditions. We had to report in daily to our website and report to our followers how we were progressing, and we would take turns to do this, so every third day I would be on. We would report on the temperatures, the wind, conditions and generally on what we were doing throughout the day.

As we were in the North Pole, and this is where Father Christmas lives, my children had asked me to give him a letter for Christmas and say hello. We worked on a little 'skit' which we published on YouTube and on the phone. We had been building up to seeing Father Christmas and at the end of most days would report that we had seen reindeer droppings (were they Santa's reindeer?), or found some old red cloth

Crossing obstacles on the frozen ocean

(perhaps this had torn off Father Christmas' coat?). We thought about how best to do our skit, and would have a right laugh together about it. In the end, Mark Wood was to dress up as Father Christmas with a beard and red hat, shoving his head into the tent, and then I would read out my son's Christmas list and discuss other things, which included mentioning all our sponsors by pointing out our food, etc, and offering them to Father Christmas. It was a good laugh, and we enjoyed doing it. It was great for team morale and the public loved it. Thinking about it, it also distracted us during our long days on ice.

Finally, we did our audio broadcast, and Mark Wood was dressed as Santa, where we did a special message to Hugo [my son] and all of the other children – this we filmed and we had a right laugh about it, I hope it goes down well to our listeners. Anyway, my back is aching writing this (hence scruffy and rushed) and I'm ready for bed. Final push tomorrow.

Reading Hugo's letter to Father Christmas

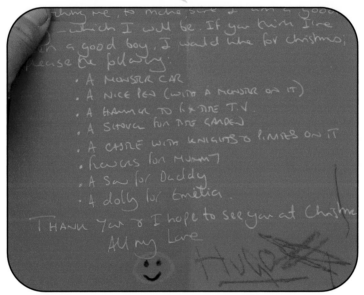

One silver lining in the North Pole cloud was that every morning, when I got the GPS watch out to check our position, we would discover that, in fact, our position had improved due to drift. Drift is caused by the current of the Arctic Ocean – either positively (with the current) or negatively (against the current). Overnight, the positive drift at the North

Communication

'Communication' refers to our own internal team communication and our external technological communication equipment.

Firstly, technological communication was key to success whilst on ice, providing protection and linking us all together with the outside world, particularly in the case of an emergency, something which would have been impossible back in the polar era.

Initiating an emergency and not having the means to communicate properly would have been irresponsible, as it would risk the lives of other people rescuing us, the lives of our team, in addition to the embarrassment and the loss of credibility, and all-in-all mission failure. Therefore, we each carried an item with which we could communicate in the event of an emergency, including two satellite phones and an emergency beacon. Should we ever lose one of the items we always had some form of back up, a redundancy which was important in such a remote environment.

I carried the beacon which could also track our route and be used for our website to update our location and progress. The beacon had a simple button to press in an emergency, which I was always conscious of and therefore covered it with tape in case I pressed it by accident. That would be very expensive and embarrassing! Both Marks had satellite phones and we all carried a number of batteries to ensure that we always had some which were sufficiently charged via solar power. These phones were our emergency back stop, but we also used them for our daily updates with the Russians, and they were our link to the outside world and our way of updating the website with information. We would send a recorded message to a storage provider where it would then get picked up and placed on our website as an audio update.

Secondly, team communication is also very important. This varied as we travelled and endured the 'white treadmill'. During training we practised our drills, knowing what each other's roles were and how to move on ice. However, you still need to be able to talk to each other, but in polar extremes, not only the environment and weather impacts on communication, but also your psychological emotions and whether you want to talk or not. To be honest, a lot of our social talking was done in the tent. When moving on ice we would be discussing which way to go, move or something about the mission in hand.

My quote, 'Together as a team but alone with one's thoughts', is very true but may seem strange because we were three people together. As previously mentioned, we would stop for a break after approximately an hour, using this time to eat our much-needed snacks and to hydrate ourselves. However, one thing which was important on ice was the ability to use hand signals. These are used heavily in the military to good effect, and work well on ice, where body language plays for 80% of all communication. So, we used our ski poles, directed by the guy at the front. It was quite simple:

- Crossed ski pole was an obstacle to my front (which could be crossing ice etc).
- One ski pole out would be the five-minute call until we stopped for a break, warning those behind. This was sometimes a good sight to see, particularly at the end of the day on your last shift.
- Two ski poles out would mean stop and have a break, when the next guy would either move to his left or right, and vice versa, for the guys at the rear.

These simple but effective hand signals worked very well and reduced any need to talk or shout. In fact, most of the time we would not have been able to hear anyway.

After months on ice, you would often have very little to say to your team mates, having run out of conversation. Your focus would simply be on nutrition and hydration. Quite often we would say just a few words, or even just look at each other (understanding the difficulties) and then pack up and walk on again.

However, when in the tent, we would, of course, talk to each other, relieved to be in the protection of our tent and that the day was over. We also had energy and wanted to talk, sharing 'banter', discussing and reflecting on the day and looking ahead. Most of this would be when we

HAND SIGNAL COMMUNICATION

TWO ARMS OUT
STOP FOR A BREAK

ONE ARM OUT
5 MINS TO BREAK

SKI POLES CROSSED
DANGER OBSTACLE

were relaxed and often in our sleeping bags with our pipes. I dare say, 'back in the day', this was very much the same.

We would also have to communicate to the outside world and the general public, our followers, via our sat phone, about how we had done that day, our distance, the weather, what we had faced and any other relevant remarks. Further to this we would have to call the Russians in Barneo and let them know that we were ok, giving our longitude and latitude position so that they could track us in an emergency. They would also provide us with any information, such as bad weather fronts, etc. Quite often it would be bad news in some form.

So, communication is vital for any team in reaching your goal.

Pole would have pushed us a few miles in the right direction. It's worth remembering that if we had travelled from Russia, as initially intended with Plan B, we would have then been drifting the wrong way, which would have had a very negative impact on morale every morning. So, there was at least one positive of the revised plan!

Our approach to the North Pole had been particularly challenging, across endless fields of broken blocks of ice, much as if an enemy had known that we were coming and placed rings of barbed wire out to hamper our progress. We were ploughing through some of the worst terrain we had ever seen, but we fought our way through it, and ML in particular could break his way through some pretty horrible areas, with his sheer force and determination.

> *24th April 2016*
> *Usual routine – mildish day really and off we went on our new adjusted bearing, hoping it would be an easy day getting some mileage in – if only we knew what was in store… we hit obstacle after obstacle of walls of ice initially to cross – finding suitable routes and the usual dragging of our pulks by hand – hard work. This was just the start… we hit more rubble, large amounts of disruption going around and winding our way though. My leg, I have to say, was the hardest so far for me and it sapped every drop of energy from me and glad to hand over to Mark L for the last leg. We then faced a massive open lead of water and luckily it was frozen so we gambled a crossing which we did; this was surreal, as it felt like I was on a boat looking at all of the icebergs, quite pretty and scenic, but also a bit scary… we made it to what you would call dry land and a few hundred metres we pitched our tent exhausted again – it really is unforgiving and unrelenting here – every day!*

For our very last day on ice we did not, in fact, have that many miles left to cover, but we had to reach the location at a specific time that the Russians were going to pick us up. So with only six or seven nautical miles to ski, we rose early with a spring in our step.

By the way, people do not always realise that the North Pole location is different for everyone, varying by degrees each and every day, and so the same was true for us. The Pole is located on a floating ocean, and we were constantly moving, like being on a boat. So if we stopped, for instance, at the North Pole, we would shortly drift away from it, and hence every Pole is different. Unlike the South Pole, there are no buildings, there is just nothingness!

The last day getting to the Pole was probably one of the hardest, as if someone knew this and was constantly placing larger obstacles in our way. I remember seeing an area which I thought was the Pole and it was surrounded by a fortress of ice! Would this ever stop? In fact, I'd say it was more messed up at the Pole than where we had been dropped off. Surely that's not right?

As we got close to what we thought was the North Pole, I consulted my GPS watch and ran around trying to find the specific location. There is a great picture of me holding the watch up and exclaiming with excitement. When we found the Pole, we took some product placement

Marking the Pole with my watch

photographs for our sponsors and then set up our tent for refuge whilst we waited to be picked up. We were in a happy place, mentally. With a sense of elation, we lit our celebratory cigars and had a tot of whisky whilst waiting for the Russians who were supposedly on their way that afternoon.

We stayed in the tent because it was (obviously) cold, and we waited… and waited… and waited, until we started getting worried. We were there for hours, so we got in touch with the Russian team and asked, "Are you coming?" They replied positively, but they had been delayed because they were picking up another group (from 'their' North Pole), and they would be with us soon. Eventually, they picked us up at about 8.00pm. In that time we had drifted two miles across the ocean from our original position at the Pole.

25th April 2016

I write this sitting back in the tent!! But, we have made it to the North Pole – yippee!! We set off early this morning, getting up at 5am, and then away for 7am; this was just in case we had any problems en route and to ensure we got to do the photos at the Pole and get on the proposed hele for 1300hrs. A good job we did, as it was again an epic to locate the Pole and get there as it led us up and over more ice rubble, weaving our way around everything, sapping my every last drop of energy. It took 3 legs of 1hr to reach the Pole – hard work. But we made it and have had an amazing adventure.

So, this is where I now sit… waiting to get off the ice and to be honest I'll be glad. I have cold feet, but sit in my sleeping bag after a celebratory cigar, whisky, coffee. We are now reflecting on what we have actually achieved – both Poles!! I have called my lovely wife, my soul-mate and support, without this, it would not have been for me. For that, thanks my love. Anyway, we sit here now stinking and looking forward to civilisation, and to let people know what we achieved. So, we achieved from 88°, 150 miles in 13 days – not bad going I think… by the way, if you didn't know, there is nothing at the Pole!

Enjoying my cigar after reaching the Pole

Mark L and myself ready to leave

"...as we looked down we saw the horrendous impact of the climate crisis"

When the Russians did eventually arrive, we had to wait in the helicopter whilst they were doing some Russian flag-waving of some sort. As I sat there in the aircraft, I felt literally chilled to the bone. All that hard work of the previous three weeks had been lost in an instance as I sat in the warmth of the helicopter. Jumping outside again to relieve myself, I felt stripped down to my bare bones, desperately cold again, and thought I never wanted to return to that place again.

We were flown back to Barneo Ice Station, but as we looked down we saw the horrendous impact of the climate crisis. It was awful, with large cracks, broken ice, and simply open water, all across what was supposed to be the ice-locked North Pole. It was just messed up out there, like a battlefield, and it crossed my mind that we were flying out in a helicopter post-mission, looking down at the devastation and destruction left behind after a military encounter, just like those battlefields I have witnessed on many occasions.

We arrived back safely at the camp where the aircraft was waiting. Everyone was rushing to board this aircraft and there was a sense of urgency to get us all off the ice in time. It felt as if the 'enemy' was closing in, like something from the film 'Platoon', and we had to get on that flight and get out of there as soon as possible. The plane was jam-packed full, we buckled up and soon the jets zoomed us away. I was so glad to get away. I wasn't scared as such, but I just had a great sense of relief to be off the Arctic Ocean and heading towards a place of safety. We were lucky to have achieved our mission. I also think we were lucky not to have had any accidents, coming back unscathed, being alive, and to have completed our objective of documenting what we saw on ice. Believe me, it was not pretty!

We can no longer exploit the resources of this earth—the trees, the water, and other natural resources—without any care for coming generations. Common sense tells us that unless we change, we won't survive. This Earth Day let's resolve to live in harmony with nature.

Dalai Lama, 2020

We have sinned against the Earth, against our neighbour and, in the end, against the creator..

Pope Francis

7. Leaving the Pole and Reflections

26th April 2016
Couldn't sleep much at all last night, maybe relieved and
excited to be back… or, too much on my mind. Had another
great shower and great breakfast – nice to be back on land.

Back in Svalbard, it was good to return to 'reality'. Having achieved our destination (albeit in a different form than we had first planned), it was three years of weight gone from our shoulders. We had done it, not how we had planned, but we could now hold our heads up high and say that we had achieved something special. Although we hadn't accomplished the mission *per se*, we had made something of it.

In Norway, we appreciated the benefits of a tasty breakfast, a warm shower, and the ability to sort out our equipment. We wanted to capture the information that we had recorded, so we did some interviews to camera to document how we felt. Looking back, I can see that I was tired and a little wiped out, both physically and mentally. The past six weeks had taken their toll.

I don't think ML will mind me saying that his opinion had changed whilst we had been on ice, from thinking that this was simply a great expedition, to actually realising for himself that climate change is incredibly real. All of us had definitely raised our own awareness, and perhaps we were even a bit shaken from what we had seen. We had been involved in a traumatic event and we were now coming back to report what we had seen: mass devastation. Here is the story.

Broken ice... the Arctic Ice had become a wasteland

MW probably had a feeling of not having achieved what we had set out to do, but we all agree that the North Pole expedition was a massive success. We should hold our heads high and remember that. In the process, we had also supported charities, raised money, linked people together for work, increased awareness, and given back to our sponsors. Yet, I guess there remains a slight feeling of disappointment because we did not quite achieve what we initially set out to do.

Diary: On Reflection
This expedition has been a journey, taking over 3 years to plan, prepare and complete. The hardest part was just to get on the Arctic Ocean as you have read, through sponsorship, support etc. The Arctic Ocean today is very messed up and it is a mess to get there logistically, as is moving on it. It is a very dangerous and risky place to be, on an ocean. The risks are plentiful, from polar bears, thin ice, ice rubble, blocks, walls, open leads and ice flows to name but a few. But, to achieve as a team something of the unknown in modern-day exploration is, as Captain Scott said, "more noble and splendidly won", and this is what we did. It was down to

having a great 'competent' team, working together with a good routine. Overall, an amazing expedition achieving, albeit reduced, our mission in documenting the Arctic Ocean, which is messed up! We may be the last of a few to ever have achieved walking to the North Pole – we'll see...

Back with our loved ones, we were sucked into the luxury of 'creature comforts', from enjoying a cup of tea by simply switching a button and boiling a kettle, to watching TV, then back into the swing of good old British culture – from the hustle and bustle of shopping, to driving our gas-guzzling and eco-friendly cars. What contrasts. We were face-to-face with the task of dealing with climate change at home and people being blinkered and unaware of what is actually happening.

A party of men go forth to face hardships, dangers and difficulties with their own unaided efforts, and by days and weeks of hard physical labour succeed in solving some problem of the great unknown. Surely in this case the conquest is more nobly and splendidly won.

Captain Robert Falcon Scott, South Pole

Tent life

We should have been treating the planet as if it was a patient long ago... no self-respecting doctor would ever have let the situation, if the planet is a patient, reach this stage before making an intervention.
Prince Charles (Sky News interview, 2020)

8. So What? A Climate Scientist's View
by Stephan Harris, University of Exeter

The Arctic is changing at a rate not seen for thousands of years. Whilst it does so, the vast majority of humans get on with their lives, oblivious to the impacts of climate change in the far north. Why does this matter? After all, the Arctic is a long way away from most of humanity, and is a region most people have never seen and never will.

To understand why the impact of climate change on the Arctic matters we have to understand a little of its geography and history.

The Arctic is a place of temperature extremes; in the dark winters temperatures of -30°C and -40°C are common, and this drives the development of extensive sea ice and maintains the second largest ice sheet on Earth (Greenland) and thousands of smaller glaciers and ice caps. The summers, with continuous daylight, are generally short and cool, but in the continental interiors of Arctic Russia and Siberia, summer temperatures of 30°C are also common.

The last ice age ended globally around 15,000 years ago, but its legacy lives on in the Arctic in the form of ice sheets, glaciers and widespread, permanently frozen ground or permafrost. This ice plays a crucial role in the climate of the region, the Northern Hemisphere and also of the entire planet. To understand this requires an understanding of how the atmosphere works.

The Arctic remains cold because of the low angle of sunlight that reaches it over the year. This is called insolation. In the dark winters with zero insolation the Arctic Ocean freezes over and the landmasses are covered by snow. In the height of summer, with continuous sunlight, much of the incoming solar radiation is at short (generally visible) wavelengths and this is reflected back into space by the white sea ice and glacier surfaces which have high reflectivity (or albedo). As a result, not much heating of the ground or lower atmosphere is achieved.

However, for a long time climate scientists have predicted that global warming would preferentially warm the Arctic and this is because of the operation of feedbacks. As global warming increases, snow, land ice and sea ice melt a little. This means that in summer the incoming solar radiation is not all reflected back to space because the albedo is reduced; some of it is absorbed by the darker ground and sea surfaces. Some of this radiates back to space as long-wave radiation (and contributes to the greenhouse effect) and also warms the air and ground further. This extra warming melts even more ice and snow, and this lowers the surrounding albedo, driving even more warming. This is, therefore, a positive feedback where the initial warming creates melting which generates even more warming.

Other feedbacks exist too, although these are less important than the albedo term. However, some of these other feedbacks may well increase in importance over time. For instance, during the last ice age, as the ground froze to form permafrost, this reached hundreds of metres in depth and currently underlies around 50% of Canada and most of northern Russia. As the climate warms, this permafrost is slowly melting and the organic material which was trapped within it during the initial freezing is beginning to decay. This releases methane which is a very powerful greenhouse gas with a long-term (100-year) global warming potential of 32 times that of carbon dioxide. Over shorter time periods the potential is even higher. As a result of this permafrost melting, atmospheric levels of methane are now higher than they have been for over 400,000 years, and they continue to rise.

So what is the evidence for climate change in the Arctic and why does it matter?

The first piece of evidence is the rise of air temperatures that have been seen in the Arctic. The first climate models in the 1960s were essentially simple energy balance models and they were the first attempts by scientists to predict the likely spatial changes in the earth's temperature as greenhouse gasses accumulated in the atmosphere. They predicted that as the earth warms the Arctic would warm more than the average of the rest of the planet, and scientists called this 'Arctic amplification'. This was, essentially, a prediction of how the earth would respond to the enhanced greenhouse effect, and we can now see that this prediction has proved correct (see Figure 1).

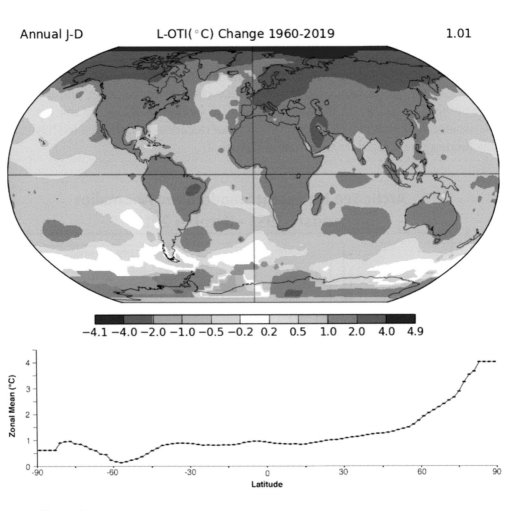

Figure 1
Global trends in mean surface air temperature over the period 1960 to 2019.
Notice that the Arctic is red, indicating that the trend over this 60-year period
is for an increase in air temperature of nearly 4° C across much of the Arctic,
which is larger than for other parts of the globe. The graph shows linear trends
over the period by latitude. Figure from NASA-GISS.

We can see that annual air temperatures in the Arctic have risen by about 2.7°C from 1971–2017, with a higher rise seen during winter, and a lower rise seen in the Arctic summers. This means that the annual Arctic amplification is about 2.4 times that of the rest of the world over that time period.

The slightly higher winter temperature rise compared with summer is caused by the later freezing of sea ice over recent decades and the melting of sea ice is the second piece of evidence. Work by sea ice scientists has shown that over the past four decades or so the sea ice has undergone a rapid transformation (Figure 2).

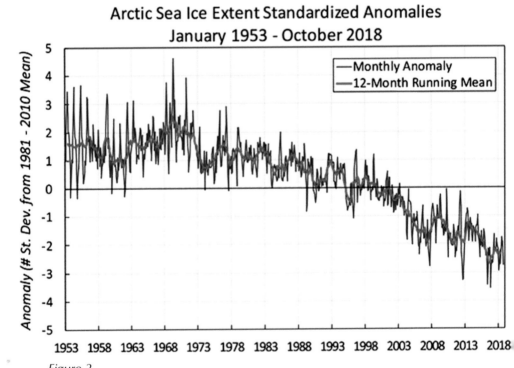

Figure 2

Mean sea ice anomalies, 1953-2018. Sea ice extent departures from monthly means for the Northern Hemisphere. The data from January 1953 to December 1979 are from the UK Hadley Centre. From January 1979 to present data are derived from passive microwave satellite sensors. Image by Walt Meier and Julienne Stroeve, National Snow and Ice Data Center, University of Colorado, Boulder.

It has changed from predominantly thick multi-year sea ice of around 3m thick to much thinner first year sea ice (about 1.5m thick), where large patches of open water are common and when later autumn freezing and earlier summer melting are occurring. The sea ice extent has also changed dramatically, with the trend in 2018 showing that sea ice extent has reduced by 12.8% per decade, relative to the 1981–2010 average baseline. As we have seen, this must have an important impact on the regional energy balance (by reducing albedo and increasing absorption of the sun's rays) but it also has a crucial impact on the behaviour of the world's oceanic circulation. This sea ice also contributes to the extreme 'quietness' of the Arctic Ocean by reducing transfer of wind momentum to the surface and inhibiting surface waves.

These changes matter to us all because the climate of the earth is partly dependent on the circulation of the oceans and the position, characteristics and strengths of ocean currents. The Arctic Ocean plays a crucial role in this by providing a water passage linking the Pacific and Atlantic Oceans via the Northwest Passage. The Arctic also drives one of the most important ocean circulation patterns and this is called the ocean conveyor or thermohaline circulation. In the Atlantic this brings warm, salty water from the tropics up to northern latitudes and takes cool, fresher water southwards again. It makes the North Atlantic much warmer than it otherwise would be; for instance, it means that northern ports in Norway remain ice-free throughout the winter.

However, with Arctic ice melt, the melting of the Greenland ice sheet and increased precipitation and river flow into the region, the Arctic Ocean waters are becoming fresher and this is predicted to slow or even stop the operation of the ocean conveyor in the north Atlantic. If this occurred the impact on areas such as the British Isles, other parts of Northern Europe and parts of North America would be profound. Temperatures would plummet over just a few years with enormous effects on agriculture, societies and ecosystems. As a result, global warming in the Arctic can, counter-intuitively, produce rapid cooling at regional scales through the reorganisation of ocean currents.

We can see, then, that attempts to bring the issue of climate change and the importance of the Arctic to the wider public are of great importance. The Arctic will continue to warm and some climate model projections suggest that the summer sea ice will have completely melted from the main part of the Arctic Ocean in the next 20–30 years. The effect of this on ecosystems would be enormous, impacting the behaviour of Arctic mammals and birds, hastening the melting of the Greenland ice sheet through positive feedbacks and the melting of permafrost. The impacts would be seen in other regions of the world too, by changing ocean currents and reducing the temperature gradient between the warm tropics and currently cold Arctic.

Few people are aware of these issues, and the role of Arctic explorers such as Vic is heightened as they have a once-in-a-lifetime opportunity to explain to the public the changes that are taking place.

Arctic expeditions such as the one achieved by Vic and his colleagues used the sea ice. These may not be possible in the future and they could be amongst the last expeditions to visit this amazing region.

We have just witnessed the warmest decade on record... As other recent reports confirm, we must act dramatically over this next decade, bringing emissions down by a factor of two, if we are to limit warming below catastrophic levels of 1.5C that will commit us to ever-more dangerous climate change impacts.
Michael Mann, Climate Scientist, Penn State University

Please make no mistake – climate change is the biggest threat to security that modern humans have ever faced. ... There is no going back – no matter what we do now, it's too late to avoid climate change and the poorest, the most vulnerable, those with the least security, are now certain to suffer.
Sir David Attenborough,
speech to the UN Security Council, 2021

9. Conclusion

At first when I heard about climate change, I was a climate denier. I didn't think it was happening. Because if there really was an existential crisis like that, that would threaten our civilisation, we wouldn't be focusing on anything else.

Greta Thunberg

As you have read, unfortunately the expedition did not go according to plan, for reasons which were beyond our control. Some may think that this was a failure, and I might not blame them... but was it? I'm managing to write this story today, which was part of our aim, 'To document what we saw on ice'. I could have written about some successes from previous expeditions, but what's important is not so much about me or those successes. Rather, the importance and relevance of this expedition to the Geographic North Pole should send a message to all of us, as together we look after our planet.

This expedition has been a journey, taking over three years to plan, prepare and complete. The hardest part was just to get on the Arctic Ocean as you have read....   *Vic Vicary*

Coming home, getting on with our lives and seeing our loved ones was so important, and such a powerful motivation. We also had a story to tell... and that's why this book has come to life, with the story that I felt had to be told. Although it has taken time, and has been its own journey facing many obstacles, nevertheless this was part of the mission, to 'document' and report back some five years later.

However, what is success, and how is it measured? Getting to the top of a great mountain… or perhaps not necessarily being able to reach the top, but instead learning from this frustration and working things out as a team as you go along. It's worth remembering that we could have simply given up at Svalbard (or in fact, back in the UK), but we didn't, we persevered, utilising some 'PESTO' and getting on with our mission. The old military adage states that 'no plan survives contact', where even the best laid plans, faced with the enemy, will be forced to change. Here our enemy was predominately the environment. We all have to be able to be adaptable and flexible, making as good a decision as we can at the time with whatever we may be faced with, even if it is a crisis…

I am not a climate scientist (although chapter 8 is written by one), so I don't blame anyone for not believing me, but what I witnessed back in 2016 on the Arctic Ocean sent shivers through myself and the team, as it should do for all of us. Something is happening up there, and it really isn't looking good! Fast forward to today and what people are facing the world over, from bizarre weather fronts to bushfires and floods, all happening right in front of our very distracted and blinkered eyes….

At the start of 2021 we are seeing the devastating impact of freezing temperatures hitting the US, with over three quarters of the nation covered by snow. Texas has been impacted worse, with reported deaths, loss of power to homes, a lack of food on the shop shelves…. something they haven't see for 70 years. This is in a powerful-first world country, where although they should have the facilities to cope, they are still struggling.

On our expedition, we were able to move from Plan A, through Plans B and C, to settle on Plan D. But is there a Plan B, let alone Plans C and D, for our planet? Will the earth give us a second chance? Or is it already too late? Let's hope not, for the sake of our children.

The clock is ticking, the issues are urgent, and change needs to happen right now. It is good to see that finally the UK government is taking a leading stance and has recently promised to cut emissions by more than two-thirds by 2030; this is a start....

In addition to all of this, as I write this conclusion the North Pole Season has been shut now for three years – in 2019 due to political tensions, and in 2020 and 2021 due to the coronavirus.

I hope this book has also helped you reflect and look at achieving your very own North Pole. Don't be put off by all those obstacles we are faced with, particularly those ones we can't control. Take one ski at a time in the right direction, reaching your tent daily for that well needed rest and replenishment, move on against the 'white treadmill', and then no doubt you will reach your very own North Pole (or learn from it). You never know unless you give it a go!

What we saw at the Pole is only part of the story, but a story that needs to be told and acted upon. Modern explorers have a role to play in observing and reporting how the climate crisis is affecting and damaging the world, bringing that information to the attention of as many people as possible. Thank you for taking time to read this book and I hope you now pass this to as many people you know and get the message out there....

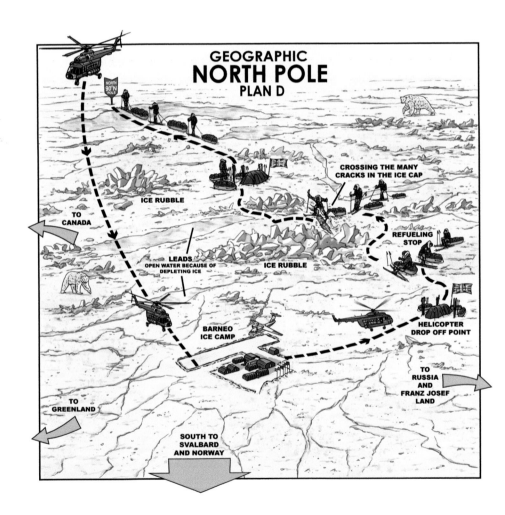

Appendix 1: Plan A to Plan D

The record of our the 'Race Aginst Time' illustrates an important military and life lesson: No plan survives contact. Our plans developed throughout the course of this expedition:

Plan A
Canadian coastline —— GNP

Plan B
Russian coastline —— GNP

Plan C
GNP —— Canadian coastline

Plan D
88 Degrees —— GNP

(see illustration opposite)

Our greatest glory is not never falling, but rising every time we fall.

Confucius

Appendix 2: **Post-Expedition Update**

This was a post-operation report written for my unit explaining what we had actually done and achieved, to enable them to learn from our lessons and recommendations.

Background

Since 2012, an expedition to the Geographic North Pole (GNP) has been in the planning. Numerous setbacks have been encountered along the whole journey, the intention being that a team of three would travel unsupported to the GNP.

Initially, during the first year, the plan was to travel from the Canadian coastline to the GNP, a recognised route, but this was thwarted when the logistics group (Kenn Borek Air) pulled out for safety reasons. An estimate was then conducted on how this could still be achieved, and a shift of focus looked at starting from the Russian coastline (supported by the Russians). Planning for this strategy continued right until the last minute (Feb 17), when we had our visas and were good to go. At the eleventh hour, the Russians refused our team transit through Russia (via border controls) for political (and military) reasons.

With less than two weeks to go, we had nothing! It was not until we were put in touch with a previous logistics support company person from the Antarctic (Antarctic Logistics Expeditions – ALE), on the back of Henry Worsley's tragic death, that we were given an opportunity and a further option – GNP to the Canadian Coastline via Kenn Borek Air. For Kenn Borek to come on board in this current climate was amazing. It was unheard of; this would be a one-off chance. The reason why only the GNP reverse plan was approved, was due to the time it would take to get back to the Canadian coastline before the ice became unstable. This was our only option and we had to go with it.

Aim

The main aim of the expedition was to document what we saw on the Arctic Ocean, so as to highlight the possible effects of climate change; raising awareness and educating people. Further to this, was our aim to raise money for charity. Most importantly for the unit was flying the flag on the 75th anniversary, with the spirit and ethos of the organisation in mind, in the most challenging environment on the planet.

Start

The team set off for Svalbard via Oslo on 23rd March, with the reverse plan in mind. The intention had been to conduct some final training in the local area, before departing on the second technical flight on or around 1st April, via the Russian support, to their ice station just short of the GNP. A short helicopter flight would then take us to our start point at the GNP, from where we would transit across to the Canadian coastline by ski.

Points to note: we were in the hands of the Russians up until 87 degrees (this includes in the case of an emergency); thereafter, we would come under the Canadians (Kenn Borek). The caveat which Kenn Borek set was that we had to be off the ice by 5th May and must have left by 10th April.

So, what actually happened?

Svalbard

As planned, we conducted the final training in the local area. This was great training and Svalbard is a great area in which to become acclimatised. We linked in with the Russians to get us out to our start point. They stated that we could get out on the second technical flight, and it had slipped back slightly to 2nd–4th April. We conducted final packing of our pulks and then were called forward by the Russians for logistics to the airport – all looked good at this stage! The ice station had been built and the first aircraft had gone in to prove the runway and drop off vital logistics. (No clients were allowed on this flight, although we did try.)

The next day, we received a phone call from the Russians informing us that the runway had cracked overnight and that this would cause huge delays due to another tractor being required (to clear the new runway).

But, they vowed that they would not give in, and continued to work on a new runway; this took another week. A meeting was held by the Russians for all the expeditions planning to leave; we weren't the only expedition, but were the only ones intending to undertake the longest and reverse route. In the meantime, we conducted further training, living out in the field and living off rations (saving costs), waiting for updates and information on when we could go. This was slightly demoralising, but we remained focused throughout.

On return from the field, we received some more bad news – the second runway that they had found had also cracked, incurring another week's delay! This was, obviously, devastating news for the team and we had to stop and discuss our options. Our only options now would be to delay the expedition for another year, or push as far as we could go and still get on ice and achieve (salvage) what we could from this mess. The Canadian coastline option was now out of our reach!

Point to note: If we delayed until next year, the same thing could happen – we could not guarantee being released, the Russians would incur a further 30% cost and we could lose potential sponsors, etc.

After a lot of deliberation and remembering who and what we wanted to achieve, we decided to stay for the long haul and see this through – getting on ice and pushing forward. We had a further meeting with the Russians (one of many) and we gave them our intentions. We were still guaranteed to be on the first flight and we had to pay further costs to guarantee our return via the Russians. We were, unfortunately, always at the hands of the Russian logistics company which was very frustrating.

The Russians stated that we would not be able to depart at least until the Sunday and we had to wait. The following day (Tuesday) we were told that it was looking good to get out earlier and we repacked /adjusted our kit accordingly. We had the call and we left earlier than planned; this was good news and a last minute bit of good luck.

On ice

We travelled via the Russian ice station at Barneo late in the evening, stopping for a brief and awaiting the helicopter. We loaded onto the hele with two other groups, getting dropped off last; we were the only team getting dropped off at the farthest point this year (88 degrees – 150 miles from the GNP). We were successfully dropped off at 88 degrees, landing early in the morning. The team plan was not to mess up our day/night routine and we pitched tent immediately to try and get some sleep ready for a full day's skiing and walking. We soon got into an effective routine, working well as a team within the tent. , Routine was key and we became 'super-efficient' after a week on ice. The extra training we conducted in Svalbard paid dividends.

The first day's walking on ice was actually our easiest day of the whole expedition, walking for six hours (seven hours including break). However, we soon hit what was to stay with us for the duration of the expedition: extremely difficult and challenging conditions – ice rubble, walls of ice and open leads of water. We had to weave our way around or through this mess as a team. Each day became increasingly difficult and messy, compared to what we had faced previously. We were now crossing open water leads and cracks in the ice, and going through huge walls of ice. All of this tested us physically and mentally.

There were several instances, in particular, where we were at high risk; we came across a huge expanse of open water and the ground was cracking around us, leads were opening up in front of our very eyes and we had to cross crushing ice leads and ice floes. Luckily, we got out of it and boxed around the area. Another example was when Mark Langridge tried to cross a lead and the edge of the ice snapped off leaving Mark in a predicament to 'tip toe' and pirouette on his skis to cross the gap safely. This he did with a cool, calm attitude – impressive! We also came across polar bear tracks twice; on one occasion they were only 500m from our tent!

The sun was our friend out there. We had to cope with 24-hour daylight, but it assisted us with our navigation (using our shadows). However, when it went out due to bad weather, we found it incredibly difficult to get a depth of perception and navigation. One time when this happened we found ourselves in 'amphitheatres' of ice walls which we had to get through – taking off our skis and dragging our pulks behind us – utterly draining! We also extended our days' marching to eight hours daily (nine hours on skis with breaks).

We were reporting to the Russians daily, but they were also putting immense pressure on the team to get to the GNP by 25th April as they would be closing down. They also mentioned that storms were coming, etc. We tried to ignore this and get on with the job in hand. What we faced every day was relentless including our final day during which, we were dragging ourselves around and through the ice walls and open leads in order to reach the GNP for pick up on 25th April – shattered! Funny old thing, we got there and the Russians postponed our pick by seven hours; this we became used to! We managed to take photos at the GNP, especially flying the organisational flag.

We have, as a team, managed to document this journey through some great photos and video footage, achieving the main aim of the expedition. This will be used in conjunction with our climate scientist to provide credibility, and demonstrate the difficulties we faced.

Summary: Planning an Expedition to the Arctic
Arctic Ocean and the GNP is, as I have briefly explained, a very difficult challenge to achieve – just to get to the start point! Ultimately, you are in the hands of external players, predominately the Russians. This is frustrating as there are never any guarantees with them. The Arctic Ocean is by far the most demanding and challenging extreme cold weather environment in the world, especially in this current climate, and the situation is deteriorating. This is not said lightly – these types of expeditions to the GNP may be a thing of the past in the not too distant future.

Conclusion
All in all, the Arctic Ocean is a mess – both logistically in getting to the start point, and whilst exploring that challenging environment.

As a team, we achieved the best result from what was presented to us. The fact that 'no plan survives contact' is very applicable here. Through perseverance we pushed it as far as we could within the ethos of the unit, and we were the only team that year to travel 150 miles from 88 degrees. We were also the only British team to get to the GNP. We achieved and salvaged almost everything from the expedition, and the flag was flown for the organisation at the GNP in the 75th year. Overall, the expedition was deemed a success.

Thank you for your support.

Regards,
Vic Vicary, North Pole 16 Team Member

Vic Vicary's NP 16 Menu List from expeditionfoods.com

Meal	Qty reqd
Breakfast	*Based on 70 days – 1 x per day*
Scrambled eggs, potatoes, mixed peppers	20
Fruity muesli	10
Porridge with blueberries	15
Porridge with strawberries	15
Hot cereal with mango	10
Breakfast TOTAL:	70
Main Meals	*Based on double bagging on day 14*
Chilli & rice	20
Mince with rice	2
Beef & potato hotpot	20
Beef & potato casserole	20
Curry beef with rice	2
Fish & potato with parsley	2
Sheppard's pie	20
Chicken Tikka with Rice	20
Spag bol	20
Main meals TOTAL:	26

Dessert
The 14 days on single rations will be supplemented with 14 days
of desserts
Custard with apple   7
Custard with mixed berries   7

Dessert   TOTAL: 14

GRAND TOTAL: 210 meals

REMARKS:
- Working on 70 days (60 days planned for exped, plus 10 days reserve).
- Breakdown = Breakfast x 70, Main Meals x 126, Puddings x 14 = 210 meals.
- First 14 days will be 2 x meals.

Appendix 4: **South Pole Kit List**

Item/ Eqpt	Weight Lb/Kg
Harness	3.4lb/1.54kg
Pulk	
Boots Alfa	5.4lb/2.5kg
	Worn On Flight (Wof)
Gps X 1 Garmin (Map 625)	0.75lb/0.34kg
Solar Charger + 4 AA Batts	0.8lb/0.36kg
Gore Tex Bivi Bag	1.48lb/0.68kg
Towel Small	0.24lb/0.1kg
Windstopper Gillet Vest	0.10lb/0.45kg
Brenig Windproof	
Jacket Outer	1.15lb/0.52kg (Wof)
Paramo Smock	
Windproof Light	0.11lb/0.05kg
Mamut Trs Windproof	1.1lb/0.49kg (Wof)
Goggles Cebe X 2	0.37lb/0.16kg
Glasses Julbo + Case	0.4lb/0.18kg
Tent Boots North Face	1.4lb/0.64kg
Sof Tool Min	
Lightweight	0.17lb/0.08kg
Camera Canon Digital + Case	0.15/0.33kg
Compass X 2 (Including	
S.Pole Compass)	0.30lb/0.13kg
Cashmere Jumper	0.8lb/0.37kg
Sewing Kit	0.34lb/0.15kg

Flask 1L X 2	1.1/2.42kg
Hip Flask (Full)	0.9lb/0.4kg
Cup ½L Thermal	0.25/0.55kg
Spoon X 2	0.03/0.066kg
Snowbrush	0.01lb/0.04kg
Kleenex Tissues X 40 Packs	0.78/1.7kg (To Pack)
Wet Wipes X 64 + Polybags	0.36/0.78kg (To Pack)
Multivits X 70	0.15/0.3kg
Snow Shovel	0.65/1.43kg (To Pack)
Skis Asnes 2m	
+ Binding & Skins	3.3/7.26kg
Spare Skins & Glue	0.9lb/0.4kg
Chest Harness	1.6lb/0.73kg
Freeloader Solar Charger	0.7lb/0.31kg
Piss Bottle	0.64lb/0.3kg
Notebook, Pencils	0.12lb/0.05kg
Mini Hacksaw	0.6lb/0.27kg
Socks Inner Wicking X 12	0.12lb/0.05kg
Leatherman Heavy	0.89lb/0.4kg
Climbing/Crevasse Harness	
& Accessories	4lb/1.8kg
Down Jacket	3lb/1.4kg
Sleeping Matt (Blow Up)	2lb/0.9kg
Crampons Steel X 2 Sets	4.4lb/2kg
Quilted Trs Buffalo	1.1lb/0.5kg
Lifa Bottoms (Heavy)	0.7lb/0.31kg
Ice Breaker 260 Merino Top	0.11lb/0.05kg
Ice Breaker 200 Merino Top	0.78lb/0.35kg
Lifa Top (Heavy)	0.87lb/0.4kg
Lifa Bottoms Lt Weight	0.53lb/0.24kg
Lifa Bottoms (Shorts) X3	0.9lb/0.4kg
North Face Thermal Top	
Lt Weight	0.34lb/0.15kg
Gloves Inner X 2	0.2lb/0.09kg
Headgear Various	0.7lb/0.32kg
Spare Felt Booties	0.8lb/0.36kg
Rollmat Ridgerest	1.04lb/0.47kg
Med Pack (Group)	3.9lb/1.7kg

Flag (Rifles)	1lb/0.45kg
Balaclavas X 3	0.68lb/0.31kg
Face Masks/Headover Various	0.7lb/0.31kg
Handkerchiefs X 3	0.23lb/0.1kg
Goggles X 2	0.11lb/0.05kg
Gloves Inner & Outer	1lb/0.45kg
Mitts Outer Vbl	0.3lb/0.14kg
Gloves Lt Weight Leather	0.18lb/0.082kg
Scott Gloves General	0.8lb/0.36kg
Gloves Marmot	0.4lb/0.18kg
Mitts Dachstein	0.57lb/0.26kg
Fleece Socks	0.5lb/0.22kg
Socks Vbl X 3	0.3lb/0.13kg
Socks Thick X 3	1.1lb/0.5kg
Military Buffalo Shirt Lt Weight	0.15lb/0.068kg
Bags Water Proof X 9	2.1lb/0.5kg
Box Tupperware (Xmas Box)	0.45lb/0.2kg
Sun Creams	0.6lb/0.27kg
Pouch Individual (Toothbrush, Lighter)	0.5lb/0.22kg (Wof)
Box Tupperware (Emergency Eqpt:Lighter)	0.9lb/0.4kg
Spare Cord	0.02lb/0.09kg
Featherlite Windproof Trs (Montane)	0.47lb/0.21kg
Flag-Tenbury School	0.68lb/0.3kg
Disposable Camera	0.32lb/0.14kg
Sleeping Bag Liner	1.68lb/0.77kg
Individual Med Kit	0.15lb/0.068kg
Pipe Smoking Complete	0.9lb/0.4kg
Sleeping Bag (Rab)	5.3lb/2.4kg
Sub Zero Thermal Top & Bottoms	0.11lb/0.05kg
Thermal Micro Top	0.4lb/0.18kg
Cycle Shorts X 3	0.9lb/0.4kg

Total to Date (22 Sep 2011)   65.77lb / 29.83kg (Excluding Wof)

Appendix 5: **South Pole Individual Medical Kit List**

Ser	Item	Qty	Remarks
01	Zinc oxide tape	1	
02	Plasters various	1 pack	
03	Betadine varnish (antiseptic cream)	1	
04	Steri strips	1 pack	
05	Compeed blister pack	1 pack	
06	Sponge toe protector	1 length	Superdrug
07	Gel toe protectors	1 pack	Superdrug
08	First field dressing (compression bandage)	1	
09	Nasal airway	1	
10	Crepe bandage	1	
11	Ibuprofen(400mg)	1 strip	Anti-inflammatory
12	Dioralyte sachets	4	
13	Paracetamol	2 strips	
14	Syringe (10ml)	1	Draining blisters
15	Syringe needles	4	
16	Diclofenac sodium (Voltaren)	1 strip	Anti-inflammatory
17	Anusol cream (and applicator)	1 tube	Piles cream
18	Sunblock (factor 30 minimum)	1	
19	Lip salve	1	
20	KY Gel (small tube)	1	For rubbing
21	Anti-fungal cream	1	

22	Safety pins	4
23	CAT tourniquet	1
24	Disposable scalpel	1

Appendix 6: South Pole Group Medical Kit List

Ser	Item	Qty	Remarks
01	Zinc oxide tape	1	
02	Plasters various	1 pack	
03	Betadine varnish (antiseptic cream)	1	
04	Steri strips	3 packs	Various sizes
05	Compeed blister pack	1 pack	
06	Sponge toe protector	1 length	Superdrug
07	Gel toe protectors	1 pack	Superdrug
08	First field dressing (compression bandage)	1	
09	Nasal airway	1	
10	Large crepe bandage	1	
11	Ibuprofen(400mg)	1 strip	Anti-inflammatory
12	Dioralyte sachets	4	
13	Paracetamol	2 strips	
14	Syringe (10ml)	1	Draining blisters
15	Syringe needles	4	
16	Diclofenac sodium (Voltaren)	1 strip	Anti-inflammatory
17	Anusol cream (and applicator)	1 tube	Piles cream
18	Sunblock (factor 30 minimum)	1	
19	Lip salve	2	
20	KY Gel (small tube)	1	For rubbing
21	Clotrimazole	1	Anti-fungal cream

22	Safety pins	4	
23	CAT tourniquet	1	
24	Disposable scalpel	1	
25	Sam splint	1	
26	Rubber sterile gloves	3 pairs	
27	Scissors surgical	1	
28	Cannula (various)	3	
29	Doxycycline	30	Antibiotic tablets
30	Loperamide 2mg	40	Anti-shit tablets
31	Ciprofloxacin	12	Antibiotic tablets
32	Co-amoxillin	1 pack	Antibiotic
33	Anusol suppositories	4	
34	Flagyl suppositories	4	Antibiotic
35	Self adherent wrap	1	
36	Chloramphenicol	1	Eye ointment
37	Acyclovir	1 tube	Lip sore cream
38	Gentisone	1	Ear drops
39	Fluorescein sodium	1	Eye colouring drops
40	Minims tetracaine	1	Eye anaesthesia
41	Sudocrem (small)	1	
42	Inadine dressing	1	
43	Celox gauze	1	
44	Cotton gauze squares	6	
45	Decompression needle	1	
46	Morphine ampoules	4	Pain relief
47	Adrenaline ampoules	2	
48	Naloxone ampoules	1	
49	Cyclizine ampoules	2	
	Controlled drugs		Carried on person in protective case (close to body)

Appendix 7:
Waiver of Liability and Indemnification Agreement

WARNING! BY SIGNING THIS FORM YOU GIVE UP YOUR RIGHT TO BRING LEGAL ACTION
UPON THE ORGANIZATORS TO RECOVER COMPENSATON FOR ANY INJURY OR LOSS TO YOURSELF OR YOUR PROPERTY AND THE RIGHT OF YOUR PERSONAL REPRESENTATIVE TO BRING AN ACTION TO RECOVER COMPENSATION FOR YOUR DEATH ARISING OUT OF YOUR PARTICIPATION IN EXPEDITION TO THE NORTH POLE.

Full Name
Address
Date of Birth   Citizenship
Describe your health in general (poor, good or excellent)
Describe your physical condition (poor, good or excellent)
Telephone number   Email address
Emergency contact name
Relationship   Telephone
Insurance company
Insurance policy number   Telephone

Preamble
The Arctic Ocean is one of the most inhospitable regions on our planet. Logistics problems are enormous; the weather ferocious and unpredictable, ice condition is unstable. Distances are immense, facilities scarce. Safety and self-sufficiency are the paramount rules. We acknowledge and respect this. It is our obligation to warn all our clients that they like us and everyone else attempting to function in this extreme

environment, are at the mercy of forces more powerful than any of us. A tight time-schedule in connection with the North Pole expedition is often unwise. Despite the expected period of calm dry weather, windstorms and blizzards along with changes in the ice conditions are a major threat to flights and groups on the route. Traveling in such a danger area as the Arctic involves high injury rate.

Initials

Disclaimer

Company VICAAT Ltd and Special Expeditions Ltd / Polar Expeditions Ltd, their agents, officials, officers, directors, employees, volunteers, contractors, servants or their representatives (hereafter referred to as the 'ORGANIZATORS') are not responsible for any death, injury, loss or damage of any kind suffered by any person during the expedition to the North Pole, caused in any manner whatsoever.

Initials

Description of Risks

In consideration of ORGANIZATORS allowing me to participate in expedition to the North Pole, I hereby acknowledge that I am aware of the risks associated with or related to expeditions to the North Pole (including the risk of severe or fatal injury to myself or others).

Initials

Release of Liability

I agree to be solely responsible for any injury, loss or damage that I sustain while expedition on North Pole and to release ORGANIZATORS of all responsibility for such injury, loss or damage. In consideration of ORGANIZATORS allowing me to participate in expedition on North Pole:

I understand that ORGANIZATORS reserve the right to refuse continued participation to any person it judges to be incapable of meeting the requirements of participation. I am in good physical condition and able to undertake this expedition.

I state that I have read the above statement on some of the possible risks and I voluntarily accept them. Therefore, I assume all risks inherent in participating in this activity, including but not limited to those listed above, for myself and my family, for bodily injury, death and loss of personal property and any expenses.

Glossary

ALE	Antarctic Logistics Expedition
AMS	Altitude mountain sickness
Barneo	Name for Russian temporary ice pole station
BDA	Battle damage assessment
Cals	Calories
CASEVAC	Military term for casualty evacuation
COA	Course of Action
Crevasse	A deep hole in the snow which can be hidden and continue for miles
CV	Cardiovascular fitness
DOP	Drop off point
Drift	Being carried slowly by the Arctic Ocean flow. This can be positive (in your favour) or negative (against). We had positive drift which added some extra miles in our favour
GNP	Geographic North Pole
GPS	Global Positioning System
GSP	Geographic South Pole
GTG	Good to go
HAPE	High Altitude Pulmonary Oedema
Hrs	Hours
Ice rift	When ice areas meet other ice areas and they collide, creating a fault which can grow to great heights
Ice rubble	Ice deformation processes in the Arctic which generate ice rubble. Many situations arise where ice fragments of varying size (some huge) separate sea ice floes
KG/kg	Kilogram(s)
km	Kilometre(s)

MBE	Member of the British Empire
Mi	Miles
NM	Nautical mile – this is a well-used measurement of distance when on ice (actually used in marine/sea). It is longer than the usual land mile: 1NM = 1.151miles
PESTO	Perseverance, Effort, Support, Time and Opportunity
Pulk	A polar sledge for moving kit and equipment
RV	Military term meaning Rendez vous (meeting point)
Sastrugi	Melted snow ice in the form of a wave
Scoff	Military Army slang for food
SMARTER	Specific, Measurable, Achievable, Realistic, Timely, Enthusiastic and Record
Spindrift	Snow spray blown across the surface of the ice/snow. Good to use for navigation
TRAPS	TNF Receptor Associated Periodic Syndrome
Union Glacier	ALE Antarctic polar base
VICAAR	Victory in Arctic and Antarctica Research
WTF	What the Fuck!

Acknowledgements

Both the mission and this book would not have been possible without the help of a whole host of other people.

I want to thank the other two 'amigos' who journeyed with me, Mark Langridge and Mark Wood, without whom none of this would have been possible.

Thanks to all the expedition sponsors and those that have kindly sponsored the writing and production of this book.

Stephan Harrison has made an invaluable contribution to the science and thinking behind the expedition and the book, and I am very grateful for the chapter he provided.

George Manley's wonderful Ilustrations bring to life so much of what we did: http://georgemanleyillustrator.com

Special thanks to my wife and family for putting up with me talking about and taking time out for 'the book'.

With sincere thanks to:

- Mark Wood for the photographs on pages xi, 3, 70, 72, 79, 84, 86, 98, 99, 105, 111,112, 113, 117, 118, 119, 120, 126, 127, 132, 136, 139, 140, 143, 144, 153, 157, 162, 164, 165, 170, 172 and 182;

- to Neil Francombe for the photograph on page 66;

- and to John the Brush (© Mark Wood Explorer and produced by Printworks Coventry) for the cartoon cards reproduced on pages 109, 150, 156 and 166.

The image of Scott on page 15 is an open license image from Wikipedia

Book Sponsors

With great thanks for your individual support for the book, without which the book may never have seen the light of day!

Book Supporters

With great thanks for your individual support for the book, without which the book may never have seen the light of day!

Natalie Allen
Clair Burgoyne
Tom Canham
Vikki Hayward
Alison Holmes
Richard Hopkins
Julia Kelly
Andrew Marlow
Darrel McGuirk
James Edward Perkins
Laura Perratt
Martin Rae
Tim Richardson
James Waring

About the Author

As described throughout this book, Vic has undoubtedly led an extraordinary life to date. He has led an exemplary 33 years' discreet military career. Alongside bringing up a young family, he has managed to find and create some key life opportunities for himself, including: being highly trained as a state-registered paramedic, challenging himself academically in achieving a Master's Degree in Security and Risk Management, walking unsupported to both Poles and leading a team of 30 women to Everest Base Camp, helping them reach their goals.

On leaving the military he was rewarded for his outstanding service with a rare meritorious medal for his dedication to Queen and Country. Vic has been exposed to all the extremes of the planet, testing his own mental resilience and mental health. He has looked the environment and the enemy in the eye, gaining key life skills and qualifications, equipping him for what is now his second career, running his own business and delivering keynote talks.

Keynotes and Speaking

The wealth of knowledge and experience that Vic can deliver cannot be underestimated. He provides fascinating and powerful talks and workshops, combining the subjects of resilience and mental health, issues which any business should be keen to address. Vic's talks have the ability to educate, inspire and protect people and the organisations in which they work, ultimately improving performance... and even saving lives.

X-Calibre Limited

As well as providing his talks, Vic also runs a successful business in delivering lifesaving training and consultancy, in both physical and psychological First Aid. This is illustrated by his logo which uses an iceberg image, as well as the brand, where his team of staff who support him are of a very high calibre. As you would expect, his company is definitely not the usual provider.

Medical Training

Part of Vic's business is delivering First Aid Training, from the basics to much higher levels, suited to each organisation's requirements. With Vic's vast array of knowledge, experience, skills and qualifications, some of which have been explained in this book, he and his team deliver quality, professional and realistic training. This can range from regulated certified training to bespoke first aid for any eventuality that an organisation may face.

Mental Health (MH) Training

Vic delivers high quality MH training and consultancy via the other arm of his business, *X-Calibre Mental Health (XCMH)*. This aims to tackle the problem of poor MH, which by 2030 will be the leading cause of morbidity and mortality. *XCMH's* quest is to raise awareness, promote a positive mental health culture, reduce stigma and ultimately save lives, something which he and his team are already achieving. Vic injects life into this arena, creating in *XCMH* a training provider which really lives and breathes mental health!

If you're interested in booking Vic for talks or his business for any First Aid or Mental Health training, please get in touch via:

paul@x-calibremh.co.uk

You can view Vic and his MH training and what they have to offer at their website:

www.x-calibremh.co.uk

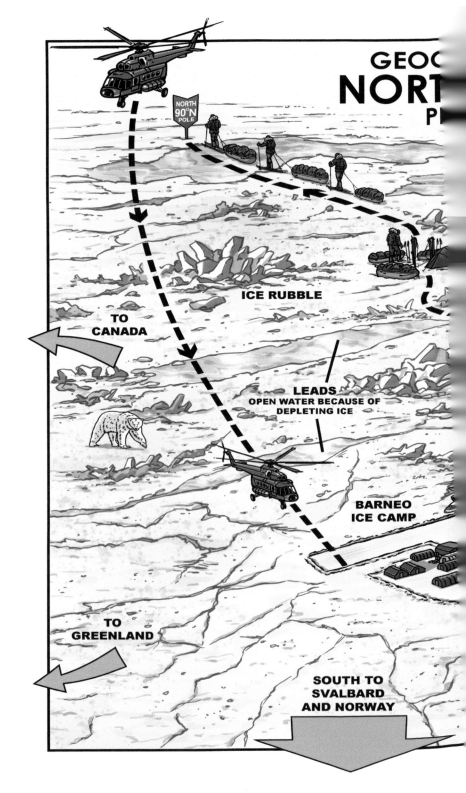